PENGUIN BUSINESS

THE SECRET OF LEADERSHIP

Prakash Iyer is a former CEO-turned-best-selling author and motivational speaker. He is also a certified leadership coach—and an uncertified cricket junkie.

In his last role, he was the managing director of Kimberly-Clark Lever. Earlier roles include CEO of Infomedia India Limited and executive director at PepsiCo. An alumnus of IIM Ahmedabad, he started his career with Hindustan Unilever Limited.

Passionate about cricket—and people—Prakash speaks and writes extensively on motivation, leadership, teamwork and winning. His first book, *The Habit of Winning*, was shortlisted for The Economist Crossword Popular Book Award, and has been translated into seven languages.

You can reach him at pi@prakashiyer.com.

PRAKASH IYER

Foreword by Rahul Dravid

THE SECRET OF LEADERSHIP

Stories to AWAKEN, INSPIRE *and Unleash the* LEADER WITHIN

BUSINESS

An imprint of Penguin Random House

PENGUIN BUSINESS

USA | Canada | UK | Ireland | Australia
New Zealand | India | South Africa | China

Penguin Business is part of the Penguin Random House group of companies whose addresses can be found at global.penguinrandomhouse.com

Published by Penguin Random House India Pvt. Ltd
4th Floor, Capital Tower 1, MG Road,
Gurugram 122 002, Haryana, India

Penguin Random House India

First published in Portfolio by Penguin Books India 2013
Published in Penguin Business 2023

40 39 38 37 36 35 34 33

The views and opinions expressed in this book are the author's own and the facts are as reported by him which have been verified to the extent possible, and the publishers are not in any way liable for the same.

ISBN 9780143419839

Typeset in Dante MT by SÜRYA, New Delhi
Printed at Replika Press Pvt. Ltd, India

www.penguin.co.in

For Savvy

'It is never too late to be what you might have been'

—George Eliot

Contents

III: THE LEADER'S WAY

Foreword

Storytelling is among the proudest of Indian traditions, and from ancient times, it has been associated with imparting wisdom and worldly knowledge. When you read the Panchatantra tales as a child, it was impossible to miss the moral underlying each story. And the Mahabharata, the grandest, the most complex and multi-layered of epics, wasn't merely a masterpiece of storytelling: it was, and remains, a discourse on life and living.

The beauty of stories is that they teach without ever appearing to do so. Most of our early world view and our moral compass have been shaped through the stories we heard in the laps of our mothers and grandmothers without us ever realizing it. We looked forward to bedtime story sessions because the tales enchanted and entertained us, and through them we learned without ever feeling the burden of formal learning. Preaching rarely works with children, and I suspect it works no better with adults. In general, we are resistant to being handed down wisdom in black-and-white terms.

Books have always been my favourite gifts, both to give and to receive, and one of my cherished memories is to be given a copy of *Jonathan Livingston Seagull* by the late former Indian Test cricketer Hanumant Singh, who was our head coach at the under-17 national cricket camp. For those who are not familiar with it, it is a fable about a young seagull fascinated with flight.

He was the exact opposite of the other gulls to whom flying was necessary only in order to eat. But to Jonathan, it was flying that mattered, not eating. It was the nuances of flying that obsessed him and while his friends and relatives spent their time searching for scraps of food, Jonathan practised flying, sometimes putting his life at risk in the pursuit of excellence. This seemingly reckless obsession leads to him being banished from the gull community but he soon finds himself in the company of a group of advanced gulls who share his passion. Under their guidance, he not only fulfils his ambitions but also becomes, in the words of his peers, a one-in-a-million gull.

It was as much a story about seeking perfection as about tenacity and staying true to the calling of the heart. The book was slim and easy to read and for an impressionable sixteen-year-old, it was a stirring and hugely motivating story. I realize now that Mr Singh was perhaps trying to convey a message to me without giving me a lecture which I might not have been keen on. It worked. And I was reminded of this many years later while reading Prakash Iyer's first book, *The Habit of Winning*.

I was primarily drawn to it because sports was a running theme in it and because I had been a first-hand witness to some of the stories he had narrated. It was apparent that he was a huge sports fan, but what I found thoroughly absorbing and illuminating was the manner in which he had dipped into the inspirational sports stories and turned them into valuable lessons in corporate life.

The Secret of Leadership is a natural and delightful sequel. Prakash has spent many years in leadership roles in some of India's best corporate houses and if his books are any indication, I can imagine him to be an affectionate mentor and guide to his colleagues.

The new book draws relatively less from sports but it has the same qualities that I found attractive in the first book—startling simplicity, lucid and easy-to-read prose and the warmth and intimacy of the narrator. The real strength of the book is that the message becomes apparent even while you are reading the stories, and you end up telling yourself, 'Hey! I knew this'. But often we are blind to the most obvious things and need to be guided to the knowledge we might already possess. Prakash does it expertly and gently. It is apparent he has researched extensively for his stories and used the wealth of his personal experience, but he fuses these seamlessly to give his books an allegorical quality.

Both my children enjoy listening to stories and my wife likes reading to them and sharing with them the tales that we have heard from our parents. As they grow older, I am looking forward to adding Prakash's books to the reading list.

This is a book that can inspire and motivate even as it entertains.

RAHUL DRAVID

INTRODUCTION

Climbing Your Mountain

At 29,029 feet above mean sea level, Mount Everest is not only the highest peak in the world. It is also the ultimate symbol of challenge and achievement. To have to climb Mount Everest is to have a seemingly impossible task on your hands. And to be atop the Everest is to experience that unique, top-of-the-world feeling.

Everyone knows that the first people to climb Mount Everest were Sir Edmund Hillary and Sherpa Tenzing Norgay. But not everyone knows that it wasn't their first shot at scaling the world's highest peak.

The story goes that after a failed attempt some years earlier, Hillary found himself back at the base camp, wondering if he'd ever make it to the top. And then suddenly, he stepped out into the sun and, looking up at Mount Everest, he screamed, 'I will come again and conquer you! Because as a mountain, you can't grow. But as a human, I can!'

Maybe Hillary wasn't really screaming at Mount Everest.

Perhaps he was just sending out a message to the world at large. A reminder that we can all keep getting better. We all keep growing. And we can all overcome life's challenges and climb all those mountains we set our sights on.

The book you now hold in your hands is born out of that belief: we can all become better. We can all grow. There's a leader inside each of us—waiting to be unleashed, waiting to climb that mountain!

Leadership is not just about the head of the organization or the captain of the team. It's about you and me and all of us. Everyone is a leader. It just so happens that some people lead teams, and some lead companies or countries. But we all lead a life. Our own. And make no mistake. How good that life is depends on the leader. On you. There is greatness inside each of us. All you need to do is reach for it. And unleash it.

The Secret of Leadership is a collection of stories in four sections. We first take a look at the leader within and draw simple lessons on the making of a leader. We then take a peek into the leader's mindset. How they think. What they believe. In section three, we look at what ordinary people do to rise to their full potential and achieve extraordinary things. What they do. And the way they do it. And finally, in section four, we look at what it takes to work with people and lead teams; how regular folks inspire themselves and those they work with, helping them discover strengths they did not know they possessed.

You could think of this book as a salad bar. There is no mandated sequence in which you need to read the stories. You can dip in and pick a story that catches your fancy. And you might even find yourself reading and rereading a story that you think is just the one for you. And like a salad bar, one thing is assured: everything being served here is good for you!

In my earlier book, *The Habit of Winning* (also published by Penguin), I had posed the question, 'If two people want to climb a mountain, what's the most important thing they need?' Is it equipment? Or training? Favourable weather conditions? Teamwork? Luck? The answer of course is that while they needed all of these for sure, the most important thing they really needed was the mountain itself. In our lives, we all need a mountain to climb. A goal that drives us to action.

And great leaders know that. They make sure they have a clear goal—a mountain they wish to climb.

In fact, the stories surrounding Sir Edmund Hillary's ascent of Everest encapsulate several of the themes that recur throughout *The Secret of Leadership*.

First, you need a goal. Hillary had that goal, that dream, that mountain. Next, your grades in school or your natural talents—or lack of them—are poor predictors of eventual success. As a child, he got average marks in school. As a gangling teenager, his limbs were almost uncoordinated. And yet none of that stopped him from doing what no man had done before. He backed himself to succeed. He persevered. He did not let failure deter him. It only strengthened his resolve. That's what true leadership is all about. Like he said, 'You don't really conquer a mountain. You only conquer yourself.'

Hillary recognized that no matter what the challenge, you can't get there alone. And so he partnered with Sherpa Tenzing Norgay who helped him achieve his goal. And that's not all. Hillary always maintained, 'We climbed Mount Everest', without mentioning which of them was the first to reach the summit. Norgay later divulged that Hillary was indeed the first to get to the top—but the leader in Hillary was never one to appropriate the credit.

Interestingly, there is no photo that shows Hillary atop the peak. He took a picture of Norgay on the summit, but when Norgay offered to return the favour, he declined. There are other photos, though, that capture the view from the top. Leaders learn to turn the spotlight away from themselves and on the people around them! For a leader, it's always about 'them'—not 'me'.

Several years later when a team aiming to climb Mount Everest left a mountaineer colleague to die so they could continue with their journey to the top, Hillary was scathing in his criticism of their decision. He slammed the attitude of wanting to climb to the top at all costs! Good leaders learn not to sacrifice their teammates at the altar of their personal ambitions.

And what did Hillary do after climbing Mount Everest? Once you get to the top, what's next? Hillary didn't just sit back and relax. He returned several times to the region and climbed ten other peaks. Later, he was also part of a team that reached the South Pole. And some thirty years after scaling the Everest, he flew a twin-engine plane to the North Pole. Wow! New challenges, new mountains to climb, all the time. Standing still is seldom the preferred option. Climbing down can be humbling and, for some, even humiliating. Which is why leaders learn to constantly set new goals and seek fresh challenges.

Hillary was a hero for the Sherpas of Nepal. Not just for his Everest achievement—but for what he did after climbing it. He set up the Himalayan Trust to build schools and hospitals in remote areas to help the Sherpas *lead* better lives. He gave of himself. And he made a difference to the lives of other people. And ultimately, that's what leadership is all about. Making a difference. To ourselves, and to the people we work with.

Think of this book as a mountaineer's knapsack. It has all the essentials you need to survive and get to the top. And instead of axes and headlamps and boots and harnesses, what you will find in here are stories. Stories to help you in your journey to conquer the mountains in your life. Stories that will inspire you, guide you and help you persevere even when inclement weather and the tough terrain make climbing the mountain seem like Mission Impossible.

As Sir Edmund Hillary showed, we can all do it. Everyone is a leader. We can all climb the mountain. You just need to believe in yourself and tell yourself you can do it. You need to take action and persevere in the face of adversity. And you need to learn to unleash the power of the people you work with, who can help you climb mountains you could never, never have climbed on your own.

Get set, then, for a sixty-story expedition. Take that first step. Your own Mount Everest beckons. Success is calling. Are you ready?

Come. You lead the way.

I

THE LEADER WITHIN

'Life is like a ten-speed bicycle.
Most of us have gears we never use.'

—Charles M. Schulz

Leadership Lessons from a Teabag!

Several forces have combined to make the workplace a red-hot challenge for leaders. It's as if someone left the kettle of water on the stove and forgot to turn off the gas. The heat is increasing and the water is beginning to boil. And leaders increasingly find themselves in, well, hot water.

With competition becoming fiercer, businesses collapsing, ethics being compromised and social media changing the rules of communication, what should a leader do? What would it take for leaders to succeed in the new normal? Given that most leaders are finding themselves in hot water, maybe we can learn a few lessons from something that thrives in hot water: the humble teabag.

Do you know how the teabag was born? Thomas Sullivan, a tea merchant in New York, created the teabag almost by accident. He put some samples of his tea into exquisite silk bags and sent them to friends. One friend didn't bother to pull out the tea from the bag and just dunked it into hot water. He loved the tea. And an idea was born!

It's probably true of a lot of great ideas around us. They were created by accident, not design. They came to life because someone dared to do something different. As you sip your next cup of tea, here are some leadership lessons to take away from the teabag. Lessons to help make your life the perfect brew!

1. What counts is what's inside the teabag. You will notice that some teabags have fancy labels, while others have ordinary ones. Some have delicate silk tassels while others have humble strings. But here's the thing to remember: the quality of the beverage is determined by the tea inside the bag—not by the label or the string.

What's true for teabags is true for all of us too. The fancy titles or the qualification or the alma mater, the clothes we wear and the cars we drive—none of these really matters. They are like the label and the string. They only make you look nice. What really matters is the kind of person you are deep down. Your beliefs and your attitude—that's what defines the person you are.

The tea masters know that to make a great drink, they need to focus on the tea. Not on the label or the string. Focus on being a good human being. Fix your attitude. Get your values right. And don't fret about the small stuff. It's really who you are—at the core—that makes a difference.

2. The real flavour comes through only when the teabag gets into hot water. If you take a cup of lukewarm water and dip a teabag in it, you won't know how strong the tea is. To get the best flavour, you need to dunk the teabag in hot water. And only then will its real strength show!

Likewise, the true character of a leader shines through in adversity. How does a person behave under pressure, when he is in 'hot water'? The hot water test is a good one for judging the quality of the tea. And the true character of leaders.

3. Good teabags look forward to getting into hot water. When a teabag sees hot water, it says, 'Wow! Can't wait to get in!' Teabags love hot water, they don't run away from it. They know they were made just for this! This will give them a chance to show their true worth.

Great leaders relish a challenge. They love the opportunity to test their skills and prove their real mettle. And it's these tough spots, these challenging situations in business and the crises, that help distinguish great leaders from good ones. Leaders love challenges. Just as teabags love hot water.

So the next time you see a challenge, a tough situation,

think like a teabag and dive headlong into it. It may be the opportunity you've been waiting for to show what you are capable of. Some of us are so scared of being scalded by the hot water that we stay away from it. The fear of failure. Don't let that happen to you! Give yourself a chance to show the world what you are really all about!

4. A teabag must be porous. Imagine you have the best tea in the world and you put it into a bag that's impermeable. It won't work. You just won't be able to make a cup of tea. For the teabag to work, it needs to be porous. You need the tea and the water to come in contact with each other.

In our lives too, we cannot survive and thrive in isolation. Leaders need to be careful not to build walls around themselves that prevent people from reaching out to them. As a leader, you need to be able to touch other people. Else, all that's inside will be wasted—untouched by all the good around you, and unable to impact all that's around you. The tea was meant to mix with the water. Similarly all of us were designed to work with other people, with teams, and with society at large.

5. Teabags work, never mind where they are in the cup. Once you dip a teabag in a cup, it doesn't matter where the teabag sits. It could be at the top, on the side or right at the bottom, it will still work. The teabag's efficacy is not linked to its position in the cup.

It is a mistaken notion that leadership is only about the guy at the top of the organization. Leaders are everywhere. And you shouldn't let your 'position' in the hierarchy limit your impact as a leader. Position is irrelevant. Leaders derive their strength from within—not from a title or a position in the organization. And truly great leaders recognize that. They look for leaders in every corner of the organization.

6. Sometimes, one teabag is just not enough. If the pot is very large, then one teabag may not be sufficient to make a good beverage. It can try its best, but the tea will just not be strong enough. The solution is simple: add another teabag.

And that can be true of organizations too. Sometimes the enormity of the challenge could call for more than one leader. And leaders don't need to feel inadequate—or incompetent—when asking for help. Too often, good leaders get branded as failures—not because they weren't good enough, but because the challenge was too big for one man. Asking for assistance is not a sign of weakness. It is often a sign of great strength and self-confidence.

7. Sometimes, you need to add some sugar and milk. If what you are looking for is a cup of tea with milk and sugar, no teabag in the world can give that to you by itself. You need to add milk and sugar.

Sometimes, the business needs complementary skill

sets that no single leader can provide. Good leaders learn to hunt in packs. They find partners or colleagues who complement their skill sets and fill in the missing pieces. This helps ensure that the end result meets the objective.

8. Someone else holds the string. Always. No matter how strong the teabag is, it recognizes that someone else holds the string in his or her hands. And they can pull the teabag out and throw it away any time they like. No questions asked.

That's a humbling thought which leaders must never lose sight of. No matter how powerful a leader becomes, he must remember there is a string tied to him that's in the hands of some other stakeholder. That stakeholder may be the customer or the shareholder or the board—or just some other more powerful force. The realization of this truth can help ensure that leaders don't let power go to their heads and begin seeing themselves as lords and masters of all they survey.

9. It's all about how good the tea is. Not the teabag! Nobody ever drank a cup of tea and said, 'Wow, that was a great teabag!' He'd say: 'That was a great cup of tea!'

In the ultimate analysis, leaders get remembered not for how good they themselves were, but for how good their teams and the institutions that they built were. Too often, leaders get caught up with looking at themselves in the mirror rather than turning the spotlight on their teams, their organizations—and their results. Good leaders never forget: 'It's not about me. It's about them!'

10. Eventually, teabags need to make way and get out. Teabags recognize that once the brew is ready, they need to move on. They don't worry that if they were to move out of the cup, the tea would turn back to hot water. And they realize that if they stayed on any longer, they'd come in the way of the person enjoying his cup of tea!

Alas, too many leaders see themselves as being indispensable and overstay their welcome! They get so taken with their own abilities and greatness that they start believing that if they were to leave, the organization wouldn't survive. They get so attached to their role and their organization that they just don't want to leave. So visualize the teabag. And remember that getting out is a normal and necessary part of the tea-making process.

The next time you pick up a cup of tea, savour the flavour. Enjoy the moment. And think of the lessons too!

Just as the true flavour of a teabag comes through only when it is dipped in hot water, the true character of a leader shines through in adversity, under pressure. The hot water test is a good one. For teabags and for leaders.

Want to Be a Good Leader? Get a 'PhD'!

There is enough evidence to show that being a great leader and being successful in life have little to do with academic qualifications. So you might be wondering why you need a PhD to be a terrific leader, achieve your goals in life and be the best you can be. Yes, you read it right, we all need a PhD.

PhD is the leader's mantra for success. It stands for Passion, Hunger and Discipline! Get them all and see the difference. Becoming a Passionate, Hungry and Disciplined person can put you on the road to realizing your true greatness.

Passion: Do you enjoy what you are doing? Do you love your work? It's extremely important for each of us to answer those questions with a resounding 'Yes!' Passion helps ensure that you jump out of bed every morning and get to work on your goals. Not because you have to, but because you love to. Passion makes those long hours spent at work seem worthwhile because you are having fun, enjoying every moment. Outstanding results are not achieved through better resources or bigger budgets. They are achieved by people who are madly, wildly excited by their mission to be the best.

Martin Luther King once said: 'If a man is called to be a street sweeper, he should sweep streets even as Michelangelo painted, or Beethoven composed music, or Shakespeare wrote poetry. He should sweep streets so well that all the hosts of heaven and earth will pause to say, "Here lived a great street sweeper who did his job well".' Would they be saying that about you? Are you aiming to be the best 'YOU' in the whole world? It's nice to be able to do what you love. But it's important to love what you are doing!

Passion is contagious, hugely contagious. Watching a passionate leader energizes the entire organization. The excitement is palpable and the leader's sense of passion and joy sends a tingle down the spine of the entire organization. The result is pure magic. When a leader wears his passion on his sleeve, it's hard to remain unaffected. And everybody seems to be doing just that little bit more to make that dream come true.

Hunger: How badly do you want to win? Are you really, really hungry for success? It's when you really want something that you start to go after it, and do all it takes to get it. If you want to win, you must first *want* to win. Get hungry. And yes, no one else can feel hungry for you.

You've probably heard the story of the young man who went up to Socrates and said he wanted to get wisdom. 'Come with me,' said Socrates and took him to a river. Without any warning, Socrates pushed the man's head under water and held it there. The man did not know what was happening. He struggled for air. He thrust his head about, flailed his arms desperately seeking to get his head above water for some air. Socrates finally let go and asked him, 'What did you want when your head was under water?' 'I wanted air,' said the man. 'Right,' said Socrates. 'When you want wisdom as badly as you wanted the air—you will get it!' So how badly do you want to win? As Steve Jobs famously advised, stay hungry, stay foolish and reap the rewards.

Discipline: Once you have the passion and the hunger, you'll probably see a road emerge in front of you, leading you to your goals. There will be obstacles on the way, there will be roadblocks, and you will need discipline to keep doing the right things, time after time after time. You need discipline to stay the course. Nothing of substance was ever achieved without discipline. An Olympic gold medal-winning gymnast put it rather nicely. After yet another triumph, she was asked what the secret of her success was. Her response: 'I practised when I felt like it. And when I didn't feel like it!'

Most of us are halfway there. We practise when we feel

like it. As leaders, it's critical to show relentless commitment. There are several examples of leaders who switch on and off—showing great intensity one day and utter callousness the next. That just won't work. Success demands and rewards discipline. Slogging hard particularly when you 'don't feel like it' is often the key to success.

That's it, then. Never mind what you are doing now, commit yourself to imbibing the traits common to all achievers and great leaders. Become a Passionate, Hungry and Disciplined person.

Success is calling. Are you ready?

PhD is the leader's mantra for success: Passion, Hunger and Discipline! Get them all and see the difference. Becoming a Passionate, Hungry and Disciplined person can put you on the road to realizing your true greatness.

Life Lessons from a Baby Giraffe

Baby giraffes never go to school. But they learn a very important lesson rather early in life. A lesson that all of us would do well to remember.

The birth of a baby giraffe is literally an earth-shaking event. The baby falls from its mother's womb, some eight feet above the ground. It shrivels up and lies still, too weak to move.

The mother giraffe lovingly lowers its neck to kiss the baby giraffe. And then something incredible happens. It lifts one long leg and kicks the baby giraffe, sending it flying up in the air and tumbling down on the ground. As the baby lies curled up, the mother kicks the baby again. And again. Until the baby giraffe, still trembling and tired, pushes its limbs and, for the first time, learns to stand on its feet.

Happy to see the baby standing on its own feet, the mother giraffe comes over and gives it yet another kick. The baby giraffe falls one more time, but now, quickly recovers and stands up. Mama Giraffe is delighted. It knows that its baby has learned an important lesson: no matter how hard you fall, always remember to pick yourself up and get back on your feet.

Why does the mother giraffe do this? It knows that lions and leopards love giraffe meat. So unless the baby giraffe quickly learns to stand and run with the pack, it has no chance of survival. It also knows that the lessons we learn early on become part of our habit, our instinct, and stand us in good stead all through our lives.

Most of us, though, are not quite as lucky as baby giraffes. No one teaches us to stand up every time we fall. When we fail, when we are down, we just give up. No one kicks us out of our comfort zone to remind us that to survive and succeed, we need to learn to get back on our feet. And often, we live such protected, cocooned, low-risk lives in our early years that we are not quite prepared for the big, bad world when we enter it.

If you study the lives of successful people, you will see a recurring pattern. Were they always successful in all they did? No. Did success come to them quick and easy? No again. You will find that the common streak running through their lives is their ability to stand up every time they fall. The ability that the baby giraffe acquires.

The road to success is never an easy one. There are several obstacles, and you are bound to fall sooner or later. You will hit a roadblock, you will taste failure. But success lies in being able to get up every time you fall. That's a critical life skill that all successful people have internalized.

Learning to win in life is quite like learning to ride a bicycle. When you start to ride, you might fall and get bruised. It doesn't matter. You need to get back up and continue to ride. Fall one more time? Get back up again. That's all it takes. Learn to get back up every time you fall.

So the next time you find a supervisor or a parent kicking you, don't get upset with them. Like the mother giraffe, they may only be trying to teach you one of life's most important lessons. It doesn't matter how many times you fall. What matters is your ability to pick yourself up and stand on your feet once again.

One organization that did the mother giraffe act extremely well was my first employer: Unilever (HUL). I remember how excited I was to be joining what was then Hindustan Lever Limited. As a young MBA with a keen interest in marketing, HLL was the place to be. I was looking forward to my first day at work. I had all these dreams of getting to work on Lux and Surf, creating the next blockbuster ad and changing the world. Guess what happened on my first day at work? I got sent off to a small town in Tamil Nadu to sell shampoos and fairness creams! You were 'flown' to Chennai, put up at the company guest house and treated with the kind of respect you thought freshly minted MBAs deserved. And then you began your stint as a frontline salesman. You took the train, stayed in lodges like the salesmen did—on a salesman's allowances—and lived the life of a salesman. Unilever ensured that every new management trainee learned a vital lesson: great marketing ideas are born in the marketplace—not inside boardrooms. Staying in touch with consumers is priceless. And having spent time doing all a salesman does, you learn to respect the hard work, challenges and excitement that a salesman experiences every single day! The lessons learned on the field in the first eight weeks of work stay with all management trainees for the rest of their lives.

As a leader, one should learn to play the role of the mother giraffe. Handling new members of the team with kid gloves isn't necessarily a great idea. Throw that new intern into the deep end. Push him out of his comfort zone. And he just might learn valuable lessons that will be handy for the rest of his life!

The lessons we learn early on become part of our habit, our instinct, and stand us in good stead all through our lives. And an important lesson to learn is this: never mind how hard you fall, always remember to pick yourself up and get back on your feet.

Advice from the Driver's Seat

He is fifty-eight years old, rather short, bespectacled, with distinguished-looking silvery grey hair. He has spent over twenty-five years working for one of India's most respected corporate houses. I have learned a lot from him. But you won't find his name mentioned in business magazines and management tomes, and it is unlikely you would ever have heard of him. His name is Karunan and he used to work with me as my driver.

Sometimes, the biggest lessons in life come from very unlikely sources. As Karunan spoke to me one morning about his life and times, I thought young people would benefit from listening to what he had to say. Since Karunan will probably never be invited to deliver a convocation speech at a college or a keynote address at a sales conference, I thought it might be a good idea to share those lessons with you. Here, then, are five valuable life lessons from the man in the driver's seat.

1. Getting a driving licence does not make you a driver. 'I was eighteen when I got my licence,' remembers

Karunan. 'But it was only after several months of driving a car that I actually learned to drive and became a real driver.' The lesson here is that a licence is only a permit and not a certificate of authority. Just as an MBA is only a qualification, it does not make you a manager. It is only after you spend several years learning on the job that you truly qualify to call yourself a manager.

Many young people mistakenly believe that getting a degree signifies the end of their learning. Nothing could be further from the truth. A degree or a diploma—the licence—simply marks you out as someone qualified to learn from real-life experiences. It doesn't make you an expert.

2. The real world is very different from a classroom. 'At the driving school, I had learned to drive a car. But my first job required me to drive a little tempo,' says Karunan. 'The steering wheel was different, and so were the gears. I thought I had learned how to drive a vehicle but I couldn't even get the tempo started.' The world outside the classroom is a very different place. That's as true for engineers and MBAs and accountants as it is for drivers. Get ready to get surprised. As practising managers, we come across these situations all the time. Just when you think you've mastered the art of driving a car, you get asked to drive a tempo. Life's challenges always throw up something new, something different. We need to adapt and learn constantly.

3. Get your hands dirty. 'I spent nights working as a cleaner. That's when I learned all about the insides of an automobile. Knowing what's under the bonnet has made me a better driver today.' The brightest marketing professionals in the country will tell you that they learned their biggest lessons in the days they spent slogging in small towns selling soaps or colas or recharge cards for cell phones. There's no other way. If you want to be successful, work hard, get your hands dirty and go beyond your specific role. I remember Vishesh Bhatia—a former boss and an outstanding leader—telling me a little story from early on in his career. He had qualified as a chartered accountant from the United Kingdom and just started work when he was sent out to a sales warehouse in a faraway location. He says he happily sat in that warehouse and made invoices late into the night at month-ends. And many years later, as the head of a large, successful business, he realized just how much those early lessons had helped. He knew exactly what happens in a sales location, how invoices are made, the challenges, the problems, the risks and the opportunities. Many young leaders think it's not necessary for them to understand 'how it works'. They mistakenly believe that their roles do not require them to understand the technology or the manufacturing process. Like Karunan, good drivers make sure they understand what's inside their automobiles, what makes their products tick.

4. Initially, what you learn is more important than what you earn. 'In my first job, the pay was bad but the boss was good,' recalls Karunan. 'He gave me opportunities to learn and make mistakes. I banged his tempo around quite a bit. While the dents were quickly repaired, the lessons I learned remain firmly etched in my mind.' In the early part of your career don't worry too much about the pay packet or the size of the organization. Make sure you get learning opportunities. Get a boss who is a good mentor. That's priceless. When you get a chance to make those mistakes early in life, you learn lessons that stay with you forever. Also, you are then never too scared to fail. Don't box yourself into an imaginary silo. Break out and learn all there is.

5. Don't worry about which car you drive. Focus on being a good driver. 'I always wanted to drive the best cars,' recalls Karunan with almost child-like glee. 'But rather than complain about having to drive a tempo or a school van or the city transport bus, I focused on driving well. I told myself that if I did that, the good cars would come. And they did.' Now that's a great lesson. It's not about the company. It's about you. Many young people are so busy complaining about the company they work for—or the job they have to do—that they don't spend enough time focusing on doing their jobs well. Do the best with what you have, wherever you are. Karunan spent fifteen years struggling in odd jobs before landing a driver's job in one of India's largest companies. We could all benefit by staying focused on doing a great job rather than worrying about titles and promotions. Do a good job. Success and happiness will inevitably follow.

Getting a driving licence does not make you a driver. The licence simply marks you out as someone qualified to learn from real-life experiences. It doesn't make you an expert.

Run Your Own Race

You probably haven't heard of a cricketing hero called Hokaito Zhimomi.

He is a star all right, the greatest cricketer his state has produced. He's idolized by fans and is an inspiration to young players in his homeland. Now you must be wondering which country he plays for and how come you haven't heard of him. Well, here's his claim to fame. In 2008, Hokaito became the first cricketer from Nagaland to make it to the big league when he was selected to play for the Kolkata Knight Riders in the IPL.

It doesn't matter that he has never played for India. He is a hero in his own right; the village lad who worked his way to the top and became an inspiration for sportspersons in the region. It doesn't matter that after being picked for the team, Hokaito missed out on a place in the final eleven and did not get to play a game for the Knight Riders. Just being out there, practising in the playing area of Eden Gardens on match days, was achievement enough for Hokaito. Getting the opportunity to share the team bus, the hotel and the nets with his childhood idols made him feel like he was in seventh heaven. All those years of hard work spent sweating it out in the playing fields of Dimapur were finally paying off.

Hokaito himself speaks with visible pride about his journey, the trials and tribulations, and the final recognition. And he hopes it inspires other players in Nagaland to reach for the stars too. You can imagine how proud Hokaito's family and friends must have felt. They'd probably be showing pictures of their Hokaito listening intently to advice from Sourav Ganguly or standing tall next to Ricky Ponting. They'd perhaps be showing footage of those pre-match moments from Kolkata Knight Riders games to visitors. It'd probably have fleeting images of Hokaito at the nets with all those stars, being watched by adoring crowds.

Now if you think about it, there are two ways of looking at Hokaito's career. You could see him as a cricketer who was not only not quite good enough to play for India, but who also failed to get a game for the Kolkata Knight Riders. Or you could see him as the little kid from Nagaland who grew up to become the first Naga to be part of an IPL team. You could view him as a failure or as a success.

Which way would you look at him? More importantly, which way do you look at your own life and career? As a story of what you missed out on? Or what you achieved? Hokaito sees himself as a success. How about you?

Not everyone can become an India player. Or be ranked first in class. Or become a CEO. But that does not make your achievements any less significant. And surely that should not stop you from trying and giving your best. Run your own race. Don't compare yourself with others. Doing well in class is important. You don't have to rank first. Being a successful manager is big. You don't have to be the CEO. Just being Hokaito is a big enough deal. Not everyone can be a Tendulkar!

There was a Nike ad with an oft-quoted, tantalizingly powerful line: 'You don't win silver. You lose gold.' Now that's a truly inspiring line to push you to win the ultimate prize. But it's probably not the best way to measure your success in life. There will always be something bigger and better that you missed out on. Maybe as a kid you dreamed of getting a motorbike. Later, when you got your first car—a second-hand Maruti 800—you celebrated, and as you went up the corporate ladder, the titles got bigger, as did the cars. Now you could look back and feel good about what you've achieved. Or look longingly at that friend from B-school who drives that snazzy BMW 7 series and wonder, 'How come I didn't make it?' If you look hard, you will almost always find someone ahead of you. Don't compare yourself with others; just aim to be the best you can be.

Learning to find happiness is the key. It is entirely in your hands. Celebrate your success and your achievements. Don't worry about the one that got away.

Maybe there's a message for all of us in a recent study of Olympic athletes. They discovered that bronze medallists were a far happier lot than silver medallists—the folks who finished one place ahead of them. The reason? Apparently, while the silver medallists kept thinking about how they missed the gold, the bronze medallists were thinking, 'Wow, I made it and now have something to show for my efforts!' They felt grateful that at least they won something!

As you look back on your life, be grateful for the bronze you've won.

Just be the best you can be. Run your own race.

How do you look at your own life and career? As a story of what you missed out on? Or what you achieved?

Learning to find happiness is the key. It is entirely in your hands. Run your own race. Celebrate your success and your achievements. Don't worry about the one that got away.

II

THE LEADER'S MINDSET

'It's hard to beat a person who never gives up.'

—Babe Ruth

Adkins and the One-Man Band

Have you heard of Hasil Adkins? Probably not. But Hasil's life story has a message for all of us.

Adkins was an entertainer—a musician who played rock and roll, country and the Blues. He never won a Grammy Award, but he was a hero and an inspiration in his own way. Adkins was born in West Virginia in the United States, the youngest of ten children in a family of rather modest means. All his early childhood he chased the dream of becoming a musician—often missing school to spend time banging drums and strumming his guitar. Constantly crunched for cash, he taught himself to repair washing machines and cars so he could earn money to feed his passion for music. True leaders learn to rise above their circumstances. They don't allow adversity to dampen their dreams of making it big.

What made Adkins an exceptional performer was the fact that he was a one-man band. Simultaneously he would sing, strum the guitar and play the drums—with his feet! That's not all. He also played the piano and the harmonica, which was slung around his neck. In fact, Adkins would keep an array of instruments around him when he performed, and he played every instrument in every composition he sang. Quite amazing, isn't it?

Now most of us would struggle to play even a single instrument. We'd probably tell ourselves, 'I can't . . . I am not good enough.' Or we'd probably rationalize, 'Nobody can play all instruments.' So how did Hasil Adkins do it?

The story of how Adkins came to play every instrument in each of his songs is even more interesting. As a kid, he was listening to the radio one afternoon. And after a song ended, he heard the radio jockey say '. . . and that was Hank Williams'. The young lad assumed he meant that Williams played every instrument in that song! And he began to believe that if he wanted to become a music star, he too needed to be able to play all the instruments. That was it. That belief—that mistaken belief changed his life!

As is the case with all of us, Adkins's beliefs drove his actions. He started playing every instrument he could lay his hands on. His beliefs transformed his reality. We all have beliefs about what we can do—and more importantly, what we cannot do. We grow up believing in our limitations, our weaknesses. Our beliefs about what we cannot do often limit our achievements. Now imagine what might have been if we believed we could do anything we wanted!

Some of us believe we are not good at math—and the sight of numbers and equations sends a shiver down our spine. If you want to change that, the answer may not lie in math tuition or more practice hours: the change would have to start with a change in our thinking, our beliefs. We might want to run the marathon, but we believe we don't have the stamina—and so we don't even try running. Before you start practising for the run, you need to start believing that you can run. If you want to change the outcomes in your life, you need to start by changing your beliefs.

And that's true for teams too. A leader can help the team achieve its potential by constantly challenging the team members to do more, by stretching them—and helping them break through their limitations and start believing in their abilities. Adkins proved that unlike in the dictionary, in real life, belief comes before ability.

There is a multi-talented Hasil Adkins inside each of us, waiting to play an array of instruments. Primed and ready to do the impossible. The problem is, we don't believe in ourselves, our abilities.

Ask yourself the question: What is the one thing you would dare to do if you knew you would not fail? What dream would you dare to live if success were guaranteed? Whatever the answer, get to work on it right away. Tell yourself you can do it, that success is guaranteed—100 per cent.

And then watch the magic begin. If Adkins could do it, you can too!

We all have beliefs about what we can do—and more importantly, what we cannot do. We grow up believing in our limitations, our weaknesses. Our beliefs about what we cannot do often limit our achievements. If you want to change the outcomes in your life, start by changing your beliefs.

'This Is Good!'

Imagine this. You've been preparing for an entrance exam. You know getting into that premier institute could set you up for life. Your parents have been praying for this day—hoping you get admission. And then, when the entrance results are out, you find out that you haven't made it. What do you do?

Do you say, 'Oh no, this is terrible. I am doomed!'? Do you brood over it for a long, long time and blame your luck and the circumstances that conspired to keep you out?

Or do you say, 'Wow, this is good!' and move on?

What you say could actually make a difference to your life. Certainly, to the rest of your life. There is an old saying that goes, 'Whatever happens, happens for the best'. It is pointless worrying about outcomes you cannot change. Focus instead on what you can change. When you get caught up in looking back at your misfortune, you start looking for someone else to blame. And rather than working on picking up the pieces and building a new future, you start looking for excuses. When one door shuts, there is no point in staring at it and banging your head against it. Look out instead for other doors that may be opening. The next time you find yourself in that situation, pause, take a deep breath, and smile. Remind yourself about this African folk tale about a king and his friend.

The king's friend was a cheerful, optimistic person. Whenever something happened—good or bad—the friend would remark, 'This is good!' They would often go on hunting expeditions and the friend would help prepare the king's rifles. One day, the friend made a mistake with one of the guns. When the king took that gun and pulled the trigger, his thumb got blown off. Seeing what happened, the friend remarked, 'This is good!' That made the king very angry. 'No, this is not good,' he said, and sent his friend off to prison.

Some years later, the king was out hunting in a place he shouldn't have ventured into. The cannibals living there caught him and began celebrating their upcoming feast. The king's hands were tied and the cannibals began to bathe him before throwing him into the huge earthen pot that was being readied for cooking. Just then, someone noticed that the king had no thumb. As it happened, those cannibals were a superstitious lot. They never ate anyone who was less than whole. So the king was set free.

As he headed back to his palace, the king recalled the

incident when he had lost his thumb. He realized his dear friend had been right in saying, 'This is good!' Losing a thumb that day had actually saved his life. He quickly went to the prison and set his friend free. He narrated his story to his friend and apologized. 'You were right. I shouldn't have put you in prison,' said the king. 'That was bad!'

'No, no. This is good!' said the friend.

'What do you mean,' asked the king. 'How could sending you to jail have been good?'

'Don't you see?' said the friend. 'If I had not been in jail, I would have been out hunting with you. And the cannibals would then have killed and eaten me!'

So, the next time you find things are not going your way, think of the king's thumb. And whatever happens, just say, 'This is good!' You will suddenly find the world a better place. None of us can control external events. What happens can be good or bad. What you can control are your feelings and your response. You can choose to feel good—or you can choose to feel bad.

When you moan and say this is bad, the mind gets conditioned to look for difficulty in opportunity. And when you say this is good, the mind looks for opportunity in difficulty. And therein lies the difference between winners and losers.

Consider the story of Dave Carroll—a much sought-after speaker, bestselling author and customer service guru. The story of how Dave became a customer service expert is an interesting one.

Dave, a musician from Halifax, Canada, was travelling with his band on a United Airlines flight via Chicago to Nebraska. On reaching his destination, Dave was horrified to find that the baggage handlers at United had damaged his 3500-dollar Taylor guitar. We would all have forgiven him for saying, 'This is bad.' But Dave didn't say it!

Instead, he wrote to the customer service folks at United, told them about the loss of his beloved guitar and sought compensation for it. While United acknowledged that the guitar had been broken, no compensation was forthcoming. He was referred from one department to another with each person blaming someone else for the unfortunate event. After nine months of persistent follow-up, the compensation was still nowhere in sight. Now we would have understood if Dave had said, 'This is bad!' He did not.

Instead, with a little help from his friends in the band, he filmed a music video describing his experience. The song was titled *United breaks guitars*. And on 6 July 2009 he posted it on YouTube. By the end of the day, the video attracted over 150,000 hits. And by the end of the following month, viewer numbers had swelled to over 5 million. Twitter, Facebook and the blog world were all singing paeans to *United breaks guitars*. Dave was the new hero on the block.

The head of customer services at United called Dave and offered to compensate him for the loss (and requested him to pull out the video). He declined the offer and asked United to pay the money to a charity instead (which they did).

Dave now goes around the world speaking to corporates about his experience in customer service and the lessons he picked up along the way. Ever since he sang *United breaks guitars*, the cash registers haven't stopped ringing. For Dave, United breaking the guitar wasn't just good. It was great!

So the next time misfortune befalls, say, 'This is good!' And you will discover how empowering that can be. Instead of playing victim and wallowing in self-pity, the 'This is good!' attitude compels you to take ownership and do things that can be life-changing.

Stay positive. Remind yourself and your team that leadership is not about what happens to you, but about your response to those events.

When you moan and say this is bad, the mind gets conditioned to look for difficulty in opportunity. And when you say this is good, the mind looks for opportunity in difficulty. And therein lies the difference between winners and losers.

The Sower and the Seeds

As I waited in the doctor's clinic some weeks ago, a framed cartoon on the wall caught my attention. It showed a patient telling his doctor angrily: 'Don't talk to me about improving my diet. I ate a carrot last week, and nothing happened!'

That set me thinking. Aren't we all like that patient? In this era of instant noodles and T20 cricket, we are all hungry for quick results. And when that's not forthcoming, we get bored. We give up and change tracks. For true success in life, it's important to remember that we need to develop the habit of perseverance. Consistent behaviour has its rewards. Always.

You can't stop working hard just because you didn't get promoted last year. You can't stop studying just because it didn't help your grades in the last exam. Look around and you will see several people who had great ideas and tremendous ability, but somehow lost their way because they did not stay the course. They stopped trying. They gave up even before success had a chance to show up! Perseverance pays.

In the Bible there's a parable about a sower and his seeds. It's a powerful little story that goes like this:

There is a farmer who is rather ambitious, and he possesses excellent seeds. Now here's what happens when the farmer goes out to sow the seeds. As he scatters the seeds, at first some birds come and get them. What does the farmer do, then? He doesn't go chasing the birds. He just continues to sow seeds.

Some of the seeds fall on rocky land. They sprout into tiny saplings. But with the first strong wind, they droop and die. The farmer would be justified in blaming his luck. 'Why me? Why do I always get rocky land?' he could be asking himself. But the farmer would have none of that. He just continues to sow, regardless.

Some seeds find themselves trapped between weeds. As they try and grow, the weeds strangle them and shut them out. Again, most farmers would probably complain about the unfairness of it all. This farmer doesn't. He just continues sowing. And of course, finally, some of those seeds fall on fertile soil, and the farmer is rewarded with an excellent crop.

What happened with the farmer happens to all of us in our lives, all the time. We are like him—ambitious—and like him, we all have excellent seeds. We have the raw material needed to reap a fortune. But we don't necessarily behave like the farmer.

When the birds get the seeds—when we find someone else taking undue advantage of our efforts, or when something is amiss—we get distracted. We shift our focus to the birds and get busy chasing them away, rather than concentrating on our real task: sowing seeds. From farmers we become bird-chasers!

It's good to remember that in life, some seeds will fall on rocky land, or amidst weeds. And at times such as these, it is tempting to blame our fate. Don't bother. Such is life. Our task is to continue to sow. To persevere. If you do that, success is sure to come.

Sometimes, a non-seasonal flood wipes out an entire crop. Farmers are devastated. All their efforts come to naught. What do they do? Do they give up and say they will not sow any more seeds? No, they don't. They realize that to have any chance of reaping a harvest the next year, they need to sow seeds. One more time. Paying no heed to the flood. But in our lives, we are not quite like that. One failure and we look at doing something else. If we don't get results, we stop trying.

The next time you find your team feeling disappointed when success seems elusive, make sure no one gives up. Tell them about the sower and the seeds. Remind them that some seeds will fall on rocky land, get strangled by weeds or eaten by birds. Their job as sowers is to persevere.

Trying does not always guarantee success. But not trying almost certainly ensures failure.

For true success in life, develop the habit of perseverance.

Perseverance pays. When success seems elusive, don't give up. Don't blame anyone. Persevere. If you do that, success is sure to come.

The Evil Monster and the Little Boy

Do you hate your job and feel that you are grossly underpaid? Is there a subject that you despise and hate studying? Is there someone who's being rude and nasty to you all the time? Have you been wondering why things are the way they are? Maybe you should hear the story of the evil monster and the little boy.

Long ago, there lived a monster in a tiny village. The villagers were terrified of it and felt their hamlet was cursed to have such a creature living in their midst. Several men tried to fight the monster. One man attacked it with a sword, but the creature grabbed the weapon, almost magically pulled out another sword—twice as large, twice as sharp—and cut the man in half. Another time, a villager set off with a huge wooden club to clobber the monster. The monster responded by slamming the man with a wooden club twice as heavy as the one he had brought along. On another occasion, a villager tried to set the monster on fire. But the monster merely opened its mouth to swallow the fire and, in return, spewed leaping flames that roasted the poor man.

Scared by these incidents, the village folk gave up trying to fight the monster. They began to believe that this was their lot and they would have to learn to live with it. Then, one day, a little boy said he would go and vanquish the monster. The people were surprised, but despite their scepticism, went along to see the little boy take on the monster.

As the boy looked up at the giant, the monster just flared its nostrils and glared back. The people were frightened. The little boy took out an apple and offered it to the monster. The monster grabbed it, popped it into its mouth, and then thrust its clenched fist in front of the boy. Bam! As the fist slowly opened, the people were astonished to see that it held two delicious apples. Twice as red and twice as large as the apple the boy had offered.

The boy then took out a little earthen pot with some water and gave it to the monster. It took that and responded by placing in front of the boy two urns made of gold, filled with delicious juice. The people were ecstatic. They suddenly realized that the monster was not a curse but a boon to the village. The little boy smiled. And the giant just smiled back.

While the story is centuries old, the monster is still around—in colleges, in offices and in our lives. Most of our problems appear as they do because of the way we look at them. You get back what you give. Twice as much!

Is someone being rude to you? Maybe you need to change the way you behave with them. And no, don't wait for them to change; you need to change first! If you get to work every morning hating each moment you spend in the office, it's unlikely you'll do a great job. If you don't contribute, don't expect to get paid a fat salary. You get what you give. Resolve today to love your job and give it everything you have. Be nice to the college's 'Ms Nasty'. Look at math as a cool, fun subject. And you'll discover that the evil monster is in fact a benevolent giant.

It's significant that it took a little child to discover the true colours of the monster. Children don't have preconceived notions. They believe the world is a wonderful place. It's only as they grow up that the optimism vanishes and the negative conditioning sets in.

Go on. Let that child in you take over. Look at everything you dread with fresh eyes—be it rude colleagues, a tough boss or a lousy job. Maybe the monster is really a nice guy. Change the way you look at it and see the difference!

Most of our problems appear as they do because of the way we look at them. You get back what you give.

'Run with Your Mind, Not Just Your Legs!'

Sometimes one single line can make a huge difference to your life. It could be something you've read somewhere or something that was said to you. And it seems to stay on in your mind and become a guiding force. Has that happened to you?

Just the other day, a dear friend of mine—a retired brigadier—was narrating the story of how a line he heard many, many years ago impacted him deeply and shaped his life.

It was his first week in the army. He had just completed his engineering course and joined the army. Amongst his colleagues in the army were several young men who had come through the National Defence Academy. Not engineers, but men exposed to the tough physical conditioning so essential for success in the armed forces.

It was a Sunday morning. The task ahead was rather simple. They had to run ten miles. My friend recalls having started enthusiastically, and then quickly tiring out. After running half the distance, he felt he couldn't continue any longer. He felt his legs would fold up and he'd collapse. And just as he was about to give up and stop, he heard his commanding officer say to him, 'Come on, young man. Until now you've been running with your legs. Now run with your mind!' Those words seemed to work like magic. While my friend doesn't quite recall what happened thereafter, all he remembers is that he kept running. He finished the entire ten-mile run. And to this day, he often hears the officer's words echoing in his mind. 'Don't run just with your legs. Run with your mind.' It's been the motto that's inspired him through everything he's done in his life ever since.

And it's a line we would all do well to remember. Success in life is not defined by talent and physical ability, but by the mental strength to stay the course and run the extra mile. When you run with your legs, you allow the pressures to weigh you down. You allow obstacles to come in the way of your progress. You find yourself saying, 'I can't!' But when you run with your mind, you become unstoppable. Your mind says, 'I can!'

Take Soichiro for instance. He was a Japanese engineer who dreamed of a career in the automobile industry. He applied for a job with the iconic Toyota Motor

Corporation but was rejected. He remained jobless for a long time, and the temptation to give up on the automotive dream and take up a non-automotive job—any job—was huge. He then tried making scooters at home. But he had no money. His caring neighbours contributed their mite to fund his enterprise. Thus was born the Honda Motor Company. Had Soichiro (Honda was his surname) run merely with his legs, he'd have given up long ago. And a Honda may never have hit the roads.

Then there's the story of Colonel Sanders. He ran a modestly successful restaurant serving some chicken dishes—until the construction of a new road put him out of business. He decided to try and sell his unique chicken recipes to other restaurants. He met over a thousand restaurant owners and they all turned him down. But the Colonel didn't give up. He kept on trying. On his one thousand and nineteenth call, one restaurant owner agreed to buy his recipe. This gave birth to the world's first Kentucky Fried Chicken outlet. Soon KFCs were opening up all over the world. Just seven years after he started the first KFC, Colonel Sanders sold his business for over 15 million dollars. Clearly, running on your mind can be rewarding!

The next time you are staring at failure and rejection and want to quit, think of Honda and KFC. Stay the course. Don't give up. And at all times, remember the officer's line: Don't run just with your legs. Run with your mind!

Success in life is not defined by talent and physical ability, but by the mental strength to stay the course and run the extra mile. When you run with your legs, you allow the pressures to weigh you down. You allow obstacles to come in the way of your progress. You find yourself saying, 'I can't!' But when you run with your mind, you become unstoppable. Your mind says, 'I can!'

The Little Dent on the Car

I'm in love with it. It's an old faithful—a black Honda Accord—and if you heard it purr you wouldn't believe it's been on the road for over seven years now. Not only does it run well, but more importantly, the car leaves me feeling good about it. And it serves as a constant reminder of a lesson I learned some years ago.

It all started a few months after I got the car. It was brand new and I loved to keep it looking that way by working on its shine. So you can understand my anguish when an absent-minded guy on a motorbike clipped my car while I was waiting at a traffic light. The damage wasn't serious, but the marks on the fender meant the car was no longer in the mint condition I took so much pride in. I was determined to set it right immediately, influenced by the theories I had imbibed about looking for perfection. I feared that if I was okay with the scratch at the back and didn't set it right, it would be the beginning of more scratches and dents and soon the car would look like a wreck. Perhaps I was also influenced by the theory that you could tell the nature of a person by looking at his car. If he drove a car which looked beat-up, he was perhaps a disorganized person who didn't set high standards for himself! It was around this time that I read Malcolm Gladwell's view on curbing violence in New York. He said they fixed broken windowpanes as soon as they could, and cleaned up graffiti in the metro stations, and that got the message across that the authorities meant business. Hooliganism and violence declined dramatically. The message seemed clear: I must keep my car spotlessly clean!

And then I saw the video of Professor Randy Pausch's last lecture. In it he made a reference to having a dent on his car—and not thinking too much about it. His message? Don't get too caught up in the trappings and the frills. A scratch on a car is really inconsequential. A car is meant to take you from place A to place B, and so long as it does that, don't bother too much about the paint!

Two diametrically opposing viewpoints, both of which made sense. What was one to do?

It struck me that this dichotomy seems to pervade all aspects of business and life. On several issues, you will hear conflicting viewpoints. There is a school of thought that says businesses should stay focused and 'stick to the knitting'. And there is another that says businesses should diversify to avoid the risk of becoming obsolete. Whom do you listen to?

You hear how sales teams should aim to achieve their

targets. There are no prizes for 'almost getting there'—in sport and in life. And just when you start seeing the merit in this advice, someone might share this classic quote from Michelangelo: 'The greater danger for most of us lies not in setting our aim too high and falling short; but in setting our aim too low, and achieving our mark.' Wow! So what should you do? Make sure you beat targets? Or aim for that hard-to-reach goal?

And the list goes on. For almost every piece of advice, you will find someone recommending just the opposite. The trick is to find what works for you—in your specific case—and go with it. Try and understand the underlying philosophy in the advice—and choose what works well for you. What you should certainly *not* do is try and please everyone. If you go down that path, you could end up a nervous wreck. Don't get caught up in inaction, unable to pick one or the other. Look at the evidence, survey the alternatives and pick the one that you think is right. And go with it wholeheartedly. Don't keep worrying about the naysayers who say, 'On the other hand . . .' That's often the perfect recipe for not doing anything.

So how does my seven-year-old Honda Accord look now? It has a little dent on the body above the right wheel. It's been there for a while now, and I have let it be. And every time I see it, I remind myself not to worry too much about the small things. A car is meant to take me from place A to place B—and my old Honda Accord (with the scratches) does that as well as anything else! I have made my peace with the scratches and the dents. They help remind me to enjoy the ride and to make sure I am moving towards my destination—without worrying about the look of the car or how it compares with someone else's! Perhaps in an indirect way, it's taught me to look at people with the same eyes: look for what's within, look at their work, and don't worry too much about frills and appearances.

Should I get the scratches cleaned? Should I obsess over its looks? Do the dents say something about me? I don't know. And frankly, I don't care. I've made my choice and I am happy with that!

The next time you are confronted with seemingly contradictory pieces of advice, don't go into a tizzy. In life, there is seldom one right answer.

Most importantly, remember to enjoy the drive!

Dichotomy seems to pervade all aspects of business and life. On several issues, you will hear conflicting viewpoints. So what should you do? Find what works for you—in your specific case—and go with it.

In life, there is seldom one right answer.

The Frog and the TV Tower

It was just another noisy Thursday in frog world.

A group of young frogs was chatting by the side of the lake, discussing the latest news. As the frogs looked at the nearby TV tower, the city's tallest structure, they thought how wonderful it would be to be able to climb to the top, and go where no frog had ever been. 'The wind, the view . . . oh, to be on top of the tower!' said one of the frogs, and the others croaked in agreement.

They decided that the following Sunday, they would all climb to the top of the tower.

On the appointed day, several frogs gathered to watch the group try and do the impossible. As the frogs lined up for the climb, you could hear the shouts from the crowd. 'Don't do it, it's too dangerous!' 'No one's done it before, what makes you think you can do it?'

Some of the young frogs heeded the warnings and dropped out before the climb started. The rest set off nevertheless, and as some tiny frogs slipped and fell, you could hear the shouts grow louder. 'You can't do it!' 'The tower is way too high!'

One by one, all the frogs gave up. Except one little frog. That frog paid no heed to the exhortations and kept climbing higher and higher until finally, it reached the top of the TV tower. The first frog ever to get there!

The frogs clapped and croaked in delight. When the little frog came down, all of them gathered around it.

'How did you manage it? What's the secret of your success?' they asked. The frog just looked on, smiled and did not say a word. It turned out that it was deaf!

And so while the hordes had been shouting, 'It can't be done', it hadn't heard a word. It thought they were egging it on, and mistook their shouts for words of encouragement!

Can you lead your life like that little frog?

As you go about chasing your goals, your dreams and your ambitions, disregard the people who tell you it can't be done. Turn a deaf ear to the critics and the naysayers.

Is there a course of study you want to pursue, but people are saying, 'With your grades, you'll never get admission'? Give it a shot.

Is there a new business idea that's been jumping about in your head, but well-wishers are saying the market's not quite ready for it? Go for it!

And do you want to be rich and wealthy, and make your dreams come true, but are being told, 'Get real, no one in our entire family has ever made that kind of money'?

Ignore them all. Turn a deaf ear. And go for it. Chase your dreams.

Remember, what you achieve in life will be limited only by your ambitions, by the size of your dreams. So when people tell you it can't be done, they are in a sense, just testing your resolve, your commitment to your goals. How badly do you want to climb your own TV tower? And while we are all excited by the size of our dream, most of us get scared by the hard work it entails. So when someone says it can't be done, we find a convenient excuse to opt out. Giving up is easy. Getting to your goals is hard work.

There will also be moments when you are the one watching other frogs—friends, family and colleagues—trying to climb their TV towers. Be careful what you say to them. You could discourage them and stop them from working towards their goals. Or you could egg them on and help them achieve their goals. The choice is yours. As one wise man said, you can achieve any goal you desire only if you help other people achieve their goals! Now that's a great leadership lesson to remember!

And yes, did I tell you whom the frog met atop the TV tower? A bumble bee! Now, according to the laws of aerodynamics, the bumble bee cannot fly because its body weight is too high compared to its wingspan. But luckily, the bumble bee never went to school and is unaware of the laws of aerodynamics. So it happily flies!

Be like the bumble bee and the deaf frog. Find your goal, your TV tower. Disregard the sceptics. And go for it. If you can dream it, you can do it!

As you go chasing your goals, your dreams and your ambitions, disregard the people who tell you it can't be done. Turn a deaf ear to the critics and naysayers. Ignore them all. And go for it. Chase your dreams. Giving up is easy. Getting to your goals is hard work.

The Dogfight in Our Heads

If you've been listening carefully, you've probably heard them already. Those two little voices inside your head. One that's positive, optimistic, bullish—let's call it the 'I can' voice. And the other, the negative, pessimistic, bearish one—the 'I can't' voice.

One says, 'Come on, you can do it. Go for it!' And the other says, 'Oh, you unlucky sod. You won't make it. So why even bother trying!' Winners and losers, leaders and followers—all of us have the two voices jousting inside our heads. The difference lies in which of those voices is winning. Unfortunately, for many of us, when reports last came in, the 'I can't' seemed to be in the lead!

Winners and leaders have the 'I can' attitude, the confidence and belief in themselves and their teams. That makes all the difference.

How do you ensure that the 'I can' voice wins? How can we break our mental barrier that says, 'I can't'? Here's a little story that might just help you unravel the secret behind winning mindsets.

There was a man in Alaska who had two dogs, a black one and a white one. His dogfights attracted large crowds. Every week people would bet on which dog would win. Sometimes the black dog won, while at other times, the white one was the victor. One lady noticed that no matter which dog won, the owner invariably bet on the right dog and won each week. When the man retired the two dogs, the lady asked him the secret.

'Simple,' said the man. 'I always bet on the dog I had been feeding all week.'

So, whether 'I can't' wins or 'I can' depends on which thought you are feeding in your mind. The thought you feed grows! Feed the 'I can' dog in your mind. Focus on your strengths and they will grow. Or keep brooding over your weaknesses and fears, and unfortunately, they'll grow too.

How do you feed the positive thought? Think positive—even in the small everyday things in life. Set yourself mini-goals and savour the joy of achieving those targets. Get inspired by reading about achievers and successful people. Spend time with hard-working and optimistic folks and keep your distance from the sceptics and naysayers. Do that often enough and it will soon be a habit. A habit that puts you on the path to winning every day.

As you go through the ups and downs of life, it is a good idea to pause occasionally, take a deep breath and ask yourself this question: 'Which dog am I feeding today?'

Winners and losers, leaders and followers—all of us have two voices jousting inside our heads. One says, 'I can'. The other says, 'I can't'. The difference lies in which of those voices is winning. So, whether 'I can't' wins or 'I can' depends on which thought you are feeding in your mind. The thought you feed grows!

Ricky Ponting and the Art of Finding the Gaps!

You can often learn vital life lessons by listening to great achievers. Their successes may be hard to emulate, but the secret of their success could provide the trigger you need to change your beliefs and habits. Here's a little story about Ricky Ponting, arguably one of cricket's all-time greats.

Ponting is one of only three cricketers to have scored over 13,000 runs in Test cricket. He has to his credit over seventy centuries in Tests and one-day internationals. And when it comes to placing the ball and finding the gaps in the field, Ponting has been acknowledged as the complete master.

Someone once asked him the secret of his ability to find the gaps. His answer was simple yet revealing. He said, 'Every batsman surveys the field before taking strike, and usually the fielders get imprinted on his mind. He can almost see every fielder in his mind's eye. But in my head, I don't see the fielders. I only see the gaps!'

And that, as his tally of runs shows, made all the difference.

We could all take a leaf out of Ponting's book. Don't focus on the obstacles. Look instead for the opportunities. Because life in many ways is like a game of cricket. Your job is to score runs. There will be fielders out there who will stop you from getting those runs. There will be an opposing captain who will try his hardest to place the fielders in a manner that will make it difficult for you to score. Your job is to find the gaps. Stop focusing on the fielders—the obstacles. Focus instead on the gaps—the opportunities.

We all face problems in our lives. We encounter hurdles that seem to block our progress. We obsess about the hurdles and fail to observe the opportunities that may be opening up in front of us. We focus on the problems rather than on the solutions. And as psychologists have proved, what your mind focuses on tends to grow. Focus on the problem, and it will look bigger and more difficult. Focus on your ability to solve the problem—and bingo!—you will feel more empowered to take on any challenge. If your mind focuses on the fielders, it will seem like they are all over the field. Focus on the gaps—and the fielders suddenly vanish!

There's a story that a former West Indian wicketkeeper likes to tell. It's a story that, he says, changed his approach to the game—and to life itself. During a Test match, he hurt a finger rather badly while attempting a difficult catch. He was in considerable pain, and went off the field to have it attended to. Meanwhile the team had to carry on with a substitute wicketkeeper, and that wasn't helping the team's cause. The coach wanted the injured wicketkeeper to get back on the field. 'I have a broken finger,' the wicketkeeper protested. 'Yes,' said the coach. 'But you have nine good fingers, don't you? Now get back with those nine good ones!'

And here's the interesting bit to remember. In life, you cannot control where the fielders are placed. Nor can you do much about the little finger getting injured. But you can choose your response. You can train the mind to focus on the fielders—or on the gaps; on the one broken finger—or the nine good ones; on the obstacles—or the opportunities. The choice is yours!

The next time you see a problem or an obstacle, think the Ponting way.

And see the gaps!

Stop focusing on the fielders—the obstacles. Focus instead on the gaps—the opportunities.

When One Door Shuts

At age ten, Julio was a young Spanish boy with a dream. He wanted to play football for his favourite club, Real Madrid! He played all day, practised hard and became a very good goalkeeper.

By the time he was twenty, the childhood dream was beginning to come true. He was signed up to play for Real Madrid. And most football pundits were predicting that young Julio would soon become Spain's No. 1 goalkeeper.

One evening in 1963, Julio and his friends set out in a car for a night of fun. Instead, it turned out to be a night of horror, as the car they were travelling in met with a terrible accident. Young Julio—soon-to-be star goalkeeper of Real Madrid and Spain—found himself in hospital, paralysed from the waist down. Doctors were unsure if he'd ever be able to walk again. They were quite sure he would never play football again.

The road to recovery was long and painful. Julio spent the night thinking about what might have been. His mind was filled with sorrow, anger, regret. To lessen the pain, he took to writing songs and poems at night, with a tear in his eye and a pen in his hand. In order to improve the dexterity of his hand, a nurse gave him a guitar. This was the first time he had laid hands on a guitar. But soon Julio began strumming the guitar and singing the songs that he had been writing.

After being bedridden for eighteen months, Julio gradually picked up the pieces of his life. Five years after the accident, Julio entered a singing contest—and won the first prize—performing a song called *Life goes on the same.*

He never played football again. But with a guitar in hand and a song on his lips, Julio Iglesias went on to become one of the world's top singers selling over 300 million albums. Just imagine! If it hadn't been for that accident, Julio Iglesias would have probably been just another goalkeeper in Europe!

What happened to Julio that evening in 1963 could happen to any of us. A setback or an accident—or failure—can often appear to be the end of the road. But it seldom is. When one door shuts, another usually opens. It's just that we get so busy staring at the closed door and banging our head against it that we fail to spot the other door opening. Learning to cope with failure is often the first and most critical step towards success.

Never let failure impact your sense of self-belief. You are a star, with unique talents. Didn't clear the entrance exam to engineering college? Maybe you weren't meant to be an engineer. That's all.

Even Albert Einstein didn't clear the entrance exam to join a polytechnic. But he didn't do too badly, did he? Maybe there is a better, brighter career waiting for you. The trick is to move on and, like Julio, tell yourself, *Life goes on the same.*

Several years ago, a bright little boy in a government school in Kerala had a dream. He wanted to be a doctor. He did well in school, and everybody was convinced that this little boy would someday become a fine doctor. He wrote the entrance exam but failed to make the cut! He was devastated.

His parents were shocked. He went on to do a BSc and then a master's, he worked with an IT firm, and later went on to co-found a company called Infosys. His name was Kris Gopalakrishnan, ex-CEO, Infosys. Had Kris not failed the medical entrance, he may have been in some little town in Kerala today, prescribing antibiotics for a runny nose or a nagging flu.

The lesson to learn from Julio and Kris is to believe in yourself. The next time that you are faced with a failure or a setback, look out for the other door. Push it open. And go find your place in the sun!

We get so busy staring at the closed door and banging our head against it that we fail to spot the other door opening. Learning to cope with failure is often the first and most critical step towards success.

The Elephant and the Peg

Do you know what they do to keep a circus elephant from running away? They fix a metal chain to a belt around the mighty elephant's leg which is attached to a small wooden peg hammered into the ground. The ten-foot tall, 5000-kilo hulk could easily snap the chain, uproot the wooden peg and escape to freedom. But the elephant does not do that. In fact it does not even try. The world's most powerful animal, which can uproot a tree as easily as you and I can snap a toothpick, remains tied down by a small peg and a flimsy chain. How come?

It's because when the elephant was a baby, its trainers used exactly the same method. A chain was tied around its leg and the other end of it was tethered to a metal stake on the ground. The chain and the stake were strong enough for the baby elephant. When it tried to break away, the metal chain would pull it back. Sometimes, tempted by the world it could see in the distance, the baby elephant would pull harder. But the chain would cut into the skin on its leg, making it bleed, causing a wound that would hurt it even more. Soon, the baby elephant realized it was futile trying to escape, and stopped trying!

So now, when the mighty circus elephant is tied by a chain around its leg, it still has vivid memories of the pain it felt as a baby. And it does not try to break away. The elephant stands still even though it's just a chain and a small wooden peg. It recognizes its limitations and knows that it can only move as far as the chain will allow it to. It does not matter that the metal stake has been replaced by a wooden peg. It does not matter that the 100-kilo baby is now a 5000-kilo powerhouse. The elephant's belief prevails.

What's true for the elephant is also true for all of us. Organizations or individuals, we are all like the circus elephant. We all have incredible power inside us. We have it in us to take on the world. But we also have our own chains and pegs—our self-limiting beliefs that hold us back. Sometimes it's a childhood experience or an early failure. Other times it's something we were told when we were younger. That becomes our chain and peg, holding us back from doing what we are capable of, stopping us from achieving what was well within our power. It is high time then to ask ourselves the question: 'What's holding me back? What's my chain and wooden peg?'

When we are young, many of us grow up on a diet of 'Don't do that!' or 'You can't do it!' or 'You are no good!' And we stop ourselves from aiming high enough. We say, 'I can't do it because . . .' and fill in our favourite excuse. 'I don't speak English too well' or 'I didn't study in a premier B-school' or 'I come from a poor family'. Over time, these beliefs about our limitations become stronger and stronger. These self-limiting beliefs become chains that stop us from trying. Circumstances change, metal poles get replaced by wooden pegs but we don't recognize that. We give up without even trying.

Organizations too are often victims of the elephant-and-peg syndrome. Memories of a failed product launch or a diversification strategy gone wrong can scar an organization's psyche, keeping it off that path forever. Even though with changed circumstances, that idea might actually be the right way forward with a high probability of success.

Until recently, the chain and peg-induced behaviour was visible on the cricket field as well. On the lush green outfields in Australia and England, it was a common sight to see the Englishmen and the Aussies dive to stop the ball. They'd throw themselves on the ground and flash a smile as they made a valiant save. But an Indian player diving around was an extremely rare sight. Indian cricketers grew up playing their game on grounds that were hard and bumpy, with outfields that had more stones than grass. As young cricketers, they may have been inspired by what they saw on television, but when they dived, they bruised their knees and scraped their arms. And they concluded that it wasn't worthwhile to dive. That memory then stayed with them—even when they went on to play on fabulous grounds around the world.

In life we often play the role of the elephant trainer in our capacities as leaders, parents, teachers, colleagues or friends. When that happens, remember to handle your baby elephants with care! Don't be overly critical. Don't belittle them. Don't chain them to a peg!

Remember, we all have the strength of an elephant. Don't let a mere chain and peg hold you back. Introspect and recognize what's holding you back. Break the shackles of your self-limiting beliefs. It's sad when we allow our achievements in life to be determined not by our strengths but by our self-limiting beliefs.

Snap the chain. Smash the peg. Break your self-limiting belief. Set yourself free. Today! Do that one thing you're scared to do because of the memories of a failed attempt. Go ahead. Unleash the elephant within!

We all have incredible power inside us. We have it in us to take on the world. But we also have our own chains and pegs—our self-limiting beliefs that hold us back. Sometimes it's a childhood experience or an early failure. Other times it's something we were told when we were younger. Smash the peg. Break your self-limiting belief.

Mumbai's Taxis and the Woodcutter's Axe

If you've been to Mumbai, you will have noticed that most taxis on its streets are old rickety black-and-yellow cars—all probably over forty years old. But change is in the air, and the last few years have seen a sudden influx of shiny new taxis. The old Fiats and Premiers are making way for the newer Marutis and Hyundais. They are newer, nicer and far more comfortable to ride in. So it's not surprising that on a recent visit to the city, I found myself seeking out the new cabs, waiting patiently till one of those came by.

As I got into a swanky new cab, I struck up a conversation with the driver. You must be in demand, I said, explaining that I had let go of four or five old cabs as I waited for a new one. 'Quite the contrary,' said the driver and went on to explain. 'Many people hesitate to get into my cab. Because it's new and looks a lot better than all those old cabs, people think this must be more expensive.'

If you think about it, this happens to us all the time. Not just with cabs, but with people too! We let our perceptions and preconceived notions impact our view of the world. We don't always wait to discover the truth. We allow our mental stereotypes to take over. If he is a great sportsperson, he must be terrible in academics. If she is successful, she must be arrogant. If it's a nice new cab, it must be expensive!

The next time you feel that way about someone, think of the Mumbai cabs. It might help change the way you look at other people!

Do you have a colleague who you think is particularly rude? And has it happened that every time you see him, you find him saying or doing something that confirms your view? Happens, right? Maybe you should hear the story of the woodcutter and the missing axe.

There once lived a woodcutter in a little town near a forest. He set out one morning to chop some firewood, but just as he was about to leave home, he discovered that his favourite axe was missing. He searched high and low, but couldn't find it anywhere. He looked in the shed where he usually left it, but it wasn't there. As he looked up in dismay, he saw his neighbour's son lurking around near the woodshed. The woodcutter thought, 'Aha! That boy must have stolen my axe.'

As he looked at the neighbour's son, he could see a nervous, guilty look in his eyes. He noticed that the lad was avoiding eye contact and shifting uneasily from one foot to another, his hands fidgeting nervously. He was now doubly sure it was the neighbour's son who had stolen his axe.

The next day, as the woodcutter was cleaning up his shed, he was surprised to see the missing axe under a pile of firewood. 'Now I remember,' he thought to himself. 'It's exactly where I had left it!'

Later that day, he saw his neighbour's son outside the shed again. The woodcutter looked intently at the boy, scrutinizing him from head to toe. 'How strange,' he thought, 'somehow this boy has lost his guilty look. He looks like a really nice, friendly lad.'

Aha!

What happened to the woodcutter happens to us all the time. The mind plays tricks on us and influences the way we look at other people.

So now when you think of that colleague at work who hates you and is out to get you, remember it's probably not true. It's just how you 'feel'. And what happens next? Everything the person does or says 'feels' like she is out to get you.

The next time that happens to you, think of where you last left your axe. And you'll discover that people around you are nice and friendly. Remember, the neighbour's son is a nice guy after all!

We let our perceptions and preconceived notions impact our view of the world. We don't always wait to discover the truth. We allow our mental stereotypes to take over. The mind plays tricks on us and influences the way we look at other people.

The Case of the Missing Goat

Do you sometimes feel unhappy with what you have and long for something that you don't? Do you wish you had a degree, a skill or a trait which, you believe, could make a dramatic difference to your career and life?

Maybe you should hear the story of the three goats.

It all started one lazy Sunday afternoon in a small town near Toronto in Canada. Two school-going friends had a crazy idea. They rounded up three goats from the neighbourhood and painted the numbers 1, 2 and 4 on their sides. That night they let the goats loose inside their school building.

The next morning, when the authorities entered the school, they could smell something was wrong. They soon saw goat droppings on the stairs and near the entrance and realized that some goats had entered the building. A search was immediately launched and very soon, the three goats were found. But the authorities were worried, where was goat No. 3? They spent the rest of the day looking for goat No. 3. There was panic and frustration. The school declared a holiday for the students.

The teachers, helpers and the canteen boy were all busy looking for goat No. 3, which, of course, was never found. Simply because it did not exist.

We are all like those folks in the school—we may have our own goats, but are obsessively looking for the elusive, missing, non-existent goat No. 3. So instead of making the most of what we have and focusing on our strengths like all successful people do, we worry about the missing piece—our shortcomings.

In the build-up to the 2011 World Cup, you might recall, there were many who felt that while the Indian team had a strong batting line-up and an effective bowling attack, it was a weak fielding side. They reckoned that would prove to be a stumbling block. So what did Dhoni and the think tank do? They didn't let that missing No. 3 worry them too much. Dhoni acknowledged that we could not suddenly become a great fielding side. That's all. No big deal. They stayed focused on their strengths, scored a lot of runs, and bowled well. And went on to win the World Cup.

Leaders can sometimes get caught up with data and information. Before taking a decision, they want to look at all available data—and then some more—resulting in 'analysis paralysis' and delayed decision-making. They continue to look for goat No. 3. As a subordinate, it can be quite frustrating to have a leader who is obsessed with that missing goat. Whatever information you give him, it never seems enough. He always wants more!

Success arrives when you learn to make the most of what you have—and not worry about what you don't have. Happiness too is a function of this mindset. You might have noticed that some people are forever unhappy and stressed, constantly looking for a higher salary, a fancier title or a bigger car. No time to have fun with the goats that they do have!

So do the best you can with what you have and be grateful for what you get. Success and happiness will come your way. Stop worrying about goat No. 3!

Instead of making the most of what we have and focusing on our strengths like all successful people do, we worry about the missing piece—our shortcomings. Success arrives when you learn to make the most of what you have—and not worry about what you don't have.

'If It Is to Be, It Is Up to Me!'

Have you heard the story of that rather unique funeral held in an office in New York some years ago?

As employees of the firm came in to work one Monday morning, they were greeted by a solemn notice at the entrance: 'The person responsible for inhibiting your growth died yesterday. The body has been placed in the cafeteria, and will be there till 2 p.m. today.'

It was saddening to know that a colleague had passed away but there was also curiosity in the air about the identity of the deceased. The employees trooped into the cafeteria to pay their last respects. A crowd of company staff had gathered inside. 'Who is this chap who has been hindering our growth?' they all seemed to be wondering as they walked up to the coffin to take a look. One by one, as each person took a look inside the coffin, there was shocked silence—and a look of disbelief.

Inside the coffin was a mirror. And below it was a placard that read: 'There's only one person who can set limits to your growth. And that's YOU.'

When we find ourselves falling short of the success we

think we deserve, we often blame our bosses, our employers, the industry or the current favourite—the recession! Everyone and everything, except ourselves. For things to change in your life, you don't need to change your job, your company or your town. You only need to change yourself. Start now. Adopt a new philosophy for your life. Tell yourself the magic phrase: 'If it is to be, it is up to me!' It's not often that you can get a set of ten two-letter words to form a whole sentence. This one is not just another sentence, it's one that has the power to become a life-changing philosophy. 'If it is to be, it is up to me!' Just say it to yourself, believe in it, and see the difference.

The power to change our lives and chart our future lies within each of us. Resist the temptation to blame others for your plight. When you blame other people, you take away your inherent power to change, thereby weakening yourself. But by taking responsibility, you empower yourself to change your fortunes. And that single act—taking responsibility for yourself—is really what separates winners from also-rans.

Have you ever seen sailboats wander into the sea? They all take off from the same place, around the same time, and yet they reach different shores. Why is that? The winds are the same. The water currents too are the same for all the boats. Yet, they reach different destinations, because where the boat will reach is determined not by the direction of the wind, but by the set of sails it possesses.

Our lives are no different. So stop blaming the winds of your company policy or the currents of the economy. Stop worrying that you grew up in a non-English-speaking home. Take charge of your life. Change your mindset and get your thinking right. Set your sails properly. For things to get better, you need to get better. Need new skills? Invest in training yourself, don't wait for your employer to do it. I find it puzzling that while young people splurge on trendy new clothes, fancy cell phones and monthly visits to the beauty salon, they want the company to spend money on training them, on making them better employees, smarter people. 'Training myself is not my responsibility' seems to be the general motto!

For things to change, you must change your beliefs and mindset. Do yourself a favour. Stick this ten-word mantra on your bathroom mirror: 'If it is to be, it is up to me!'

There's only one person who can set limits to your growth. And that's YOU.

From Problem Child to the World's Best Ballerina

It's always fascinating to hear stories of successful people and how they got there. These stories can be hugely inspiring and often hold a lesson that can change the course of our lives. Have you heard of Gillian Lynne? Gillian is a British ballerina and one of the world's leading choreographers. She has been associated with some of the biggest hits on Broadway, including *Cats* and *The Phantom of the Opera*. Widely respected, she is a multimillionaire too. Sir Ken Robinson, an authority on education and creativity—and an outstanding speaker—loves to tell the story of Gillian Lynne.

When Gillian was eight, her mother received a letter from her schoolteacher complaining about her behaviour in school. The teacher said Gillian was fidgety, unable to sit in one place or concentrate, and was distracting her classmates too. She was late in submitting her homework, and her handwriting was terrible. 'I suspect she has a learning disorder,' concluded the teacher, advising the parents to move their daughter to a special school.

Worried, the mother decided to take Gillian to a psychologist to better understand the problem and the possible cure. Little Gillian sat nervously in the psychologist's chamber as he spoke to her mother. He looked at her intermittently, watching the expression on her face and her little legs dangling from the chair. After about twenty minutes, he told Gillian he wanted to have a little personal chat with her mother, and they would both be back in just a bit. And as he was leaving he turned on a radio that was on his desk.

As soon as the door shut, little Gillian jumped to her feet and began to dance to the music playing on the radio. There was a look of pure joy on her face as she swayed gracefully. Standing outside near a window, the psychologist asked Gillian's mother to look at what her daughter was doing. And they were both amazed to see little Gillian dancing away. 'She is not sick,' said the psychologist. 'She is a dancer. Send her to a dance school.'

Luckily for Gillian, her mother heeded the advice and did just that. And the rest, as they say, is history. She went to dance school and from there to the Royal Ballet School in London. She went on to become one of the world's greatest dancers and choreographers—a woman who brought joy to audiences around the world. Thanks perhaps to a perceptive psychologist who could see the ballerina hidden inside the fidgety eight-year-old girl. He could have put her on a course of medicines to make her less fidgety, or sent her off to a special school. But he saw the genius trapped inside that little body and decided to help set it free.

What was true of Gillian is probably true for many of us. There is a special talent hidden inside each of us. The problem is, it often stays hidden forever. We all get measured by identical, almost archaic, academic yardsticks in school. A measure that only recognizes our ability to read, add some numbers, learn by rote and score high marks. Failing to do that marks out children as failures. It marks them out as people who are not quite good enough. Which is both unfair and incorrect.

The next time you get a mark sheet that says you are not good enough, don't let it diminish your sense of self-worth. Look instead for what gives you your greatest joy. What do you most enjoy doing? What's the special talent you have that's uniquely yours? What would you like to do for the rest of your life? Finding those answers—and then working hard to follow that dream—can possibly ensure your best chance to achieve greatness.

Maybe what we all need is someone like that psychologist. We need a teacher or a parent who can spot the real talent inside us. Someone who turns on the radio and lets the music play.

What do you most enjoy doing? What's the special talent you have that's uniquely yours? What would you like to do for the rest of your life? Finding those answers—and then working hard to follow that dream—can possibly ensure your best chance to achieve greatness.

For Things to Change, We Must Change

Myra was a rather unhappy girl. She hated her job. Ask her why, and the response would be quick: her colleagues were all snobbish and unhelpful. Terrible people to work with!

Diya always walked around with a happy smile on her face. She loved her work. And if you asked her why, her response too would be swift: her colleagues were warm and friendly. Wonderful folks to hang out with!

Now you're probably thinking we are all like them. If we are lucky to be in a place where the people are nice and friendly, we are happy. And if we are not so fortunate, and find ourselves in the midst of not-so-nice people, we become unhappy.

But here's the interesting bit. Both Diya and Myra work for the same organization. In fact, they are in the same department! If you look around, you'll find several people like Diya and Myra. It could be two people who work in the same organization, or are studying the same course, or living in the same city; while one of them loves everything about the company or the course or the place they live in, the other always complains about how terrible their world is.

Same place, different views. Why does this happen? Maybe there's a message in the story of the old man who ran a tea stall on a highway between two cities. It was a popular stopover for motorists, partly because of the quality of the tea, but mostly because of the friendly old man who ran it.

One day, a group of friends travelling in a car stopped by, and after all of them had helped themselves to some refreshing hot tea, one of them asked the old man, 'How are the people in the town ahead?'

'How were the people in the town you are coming from?' asked the old man.

'Oh, they were lousy,' was the reply. 'Arrogant and ill-mannered!'

The old man paused for a moment and said, 'You will find that the people in the town ahead are also like that.'

A little while later, another car pulled over at the tea shop. The folks in the car enjoyed their tea, and as they were about to drive off, one of them asked the old man the same question: 'How are the people in the town ahead?'

And the old man responded, 'How were the people in the town you are coming from?'

'They were wonderful people,' came the response. 'Warm and helpful.'

The old man smiled and said, 'You will find that the people in the town ahead are exactly the same.'

Think about it. It's always like that. The way we see the people around us depends not so much on how they are—but on how we are.

If you find yourself unhappy with the people and circumstances in your life, maybe the problem is not with them—it's with you! If the world around you looks dark and gloomy when someone else finds it bright and sunny, maybe all you need to do is remove your sunglasses! Change the way you look at your world. Resolve to be happy. Be positive. Be friendly. And the world will seem a better place.

Become the kind of friend or colleague you'd want to have and surprise, surprise—you'll find that the people around you are like that too. You will find all the warmth and friendliness reflecting back at you. We all tend to attract people and circumstances that are in harmony with our attitude. Happy people have happy friends, happy lives. But the converse tends to be generally true too.

So as a leader, how do you see your teammates? When you look around, do you feel you have a bunch of ne'er-do-wells? Chances are that's the way they will turn out. Or do you see a team of world-beaters? If you do, you'll probably find your team doing things that might have seemed impossible. It often happens in organizations. One leader sees his team as no good, and is forever complaining about how difficult it is to deliver results with such employees. And then another leader comes along and the team seems to turn around and work like magic. It all boils down to the attitude of the leader.

Remember, for things to change, we must change. Your job, your company, your city—all these could be wonderful places. You just need to learn to look at them that way. Gandhiji's advice still holds true for leaders: be the change you want to see.

Starting today, change your outlook. Change your world!

The way we see the people around us depends not so much on how they are—but on how we are.

Confront Your Fears and You'll Conquer Them!

Have you heard the story of the Zen master and the dogs in the temple? It has a message that has changed lives.

While travelling through a little Himalayan kingdom, the master decided to visit the temple there. As he walked in through the temple gates with his local guide, he saw two large, ferocious dogs chained to the iron grilles at the entrance. They were straining at their chains, their tongues were wagging, the saliva was dripping and they were barking non-stop. Just the kind of sight that could instil fear in anybody's mind!

'Don't worry, master!' said the helpful guide. 'I know they look really scary. But the chains are very strong and there is no way the dogs can break free!' The master continued to walk down the long courtyard towards the main temple. Even as he tried to concentrate on the temple's history that the guide was narrating, he kept looking back at those dogs. The sound of their barking seemed to be echoing in his ears.

And as he looked back one more time, he could not believe what he saw. The dogs had broken free from their chains and were running towards him. Instantly the master started to run too. Directly towards the dogs! Yes, he began to run—not away from the dogs, but towards them! And guess what happened? The dogs were so surprised to see the master running towards them that they quietly turned and went back towards the gate!

Think of those ferocious dogs as symbolizing the biggest fears in your life. What do we all tend to do? We tend to run away from our fears. And hope that they will go away. Take a leaf from the monk's book and run *towards* your fears. Confront your fears—nay, embrace them—and you will find that you can conquer them!

Many of us go through our lives with a constant fear of failure. We are too scared to try new things because we are afraid we will fail. We live a life of unfulfilled potential because we are too scared to get started. Break the cycle. Face your fear. And give it a try. You will be surprised. Scared of water? Join swimming classes! Scared of public speaking? Grab every opportunity you get to address a gathering. Scared that you might fail in your dream entrepreneurial venture? Well, give it a shot and get started. Never mind the outcome—one thing is guaranteed. The fear will vanish.

Someone once said that FEAR is really an acronym for False Expectations Appearing Real. Once you understand that, you could take a big step towards achieving your dreams. Think of your fears as a wall ahead of you. Your success and your happiness lie on the other side of that wall. And yet, what do we do? We run away from the wall, away from where our dreams are. To find success, you need to get to the wall and scale it. And as you get to the wall—to your fear—you will discover that it is in fact no wall at all, just a low hedge that you can easily jump over!

If you are a cricket fan, you will probably remember the Lord's Test between India and England in 1990. Replying to England's first innings score of 653 for 4 declared, India were 430 for 9, when the last man walked out to join Kapil Dev. India needed 24 runs to avoid the follow on. With just one wicket left. The pressure was on. The threat of a follow on loomed large. Tension, fear and anxiety filled the air. And how did Kapil Dev respond? He hit four sixes in a row, and knocked off those 24 runs needed to avoid the follow on. Just like that!

That's the way to deal with your fears. Confront them. Run towards them. Or as Kapil paaji would advise you, hit them for a six!

Confront your fears—nay, embrace them—and you will find that you can conquer them!

What's Your Next Mountain?

Marcus Trescothick was a talented but somewhat unusual cricketer.

There's an interesting little story from his early days that has a useful lesson for us all. The young Marcus was making waves with his batting displays and people were beginning to rave about the precocious talent, predicting a bright future for the cricketer. And his coach knew that for Marcus to realize his potential and go all the way, it was important for him not only to continue to improve his technique, but also to be mentally strong. The story goes that in one of his early competitive games, when Marcus hit a hundred, there was much celebration. Marcus was delighted. A dream had come true. And he continued to bat well and looked set for a double century—when suddenly, his coach declared the innings and left Trescothick short of his double hundred.

The coach later explained why he had done that. He did not want his ward to feel he had achieved everything too soon. He wanted Marcus to stay hungry. He knew that it wouldn't help Marcus's development if he felt he had done it all, been there, done that—too soon.

The hunger remained. Trescothick continued to score big and forced his way into the England team. He also learned to value every opportunity—and never took anything for granted.

Stay hungry. Make sure there's always another peak to climb, a new milestone to reach and a new challenge to overcome. This ensures that we keep getting better, and continue to develop and make progress. Too often, a mistake young people make is to think they've arrived. The top-of-the-world feeling only means that every step from thereon is downhill. And that's no good.

Good leaders ensure they continue to stretch and challenge themselves and the high achievers who work with them. They keep raising the bar relentlessly.

Some years ago, the NASA folks discovered they had a problem. Several astronauts who had returned after making successful trips to the moon were plagued with psychological problems. They were struggling to cope with retirement, with post-'voyage to the moon' blues. They needed professional help. If you've been to the moon and back, what else can excite you? What's the next goal, the next challenge? Without it, the astronauts were listless and lost!

Make sure you have something new to look forward to at all times. Even as they are approaching the top of a mountain, good leaders ensure there's another mountain waiting to be climbed.

There's great advice in an off-the-cuff remark made by Claudio Gonzalez, the president of Kimberly Clark Mexico. He is the man who spearheaded the growth of Kimberly Clark's business in that country, and has seen it scale new heights even after he relinquished operational leadership. When asked if he was happy with the progress being made by the company, his response was brief but revealing: 'Happy, but not satisfied.'

That's a good mantra to have. Be happy to have been able to climb one mountain. But never be satisfied—so you keep looking for newer mountains to climb.

Time to ask yourself the question: 'What's next?'

Make sure there's always another peak to climb, a new milestone to reach and a new challenge to overcome.

Good leaders ensure they continue to stretch and challenge themselves and the high achievers who work with them. They keep raising the bar relentlessly.

III

THE LEADER'S WAY

'Start by doing what's necessary; then do what's possible; and suddenly you are doing the impossible.'

—St Francis of Assisi

The One Winning Habit of Several Great Leaders!

Guess what Jack Welch, Gordon Brown, Adi Godrej and Dr Manmohan Singh have in common?

They are all early risers. In fact, if you read about the lives of successful people, you will most likely find a common thread: they all wake up early. It's a habit that's worked wonderfully well for them. And it could work like magic for you too. If there was one single habit that could make a huge impact on your life, it would have to be this. Wake up early!

You've probably heard that every morning in Africa, a gazelle wakes up knowing it must run faster than the fastest lion, or else it will be killed. And every morning, a lion wakes up knowing it must run faster than the slowest gazelle, or else it will starve to death. The moral of the story is simple. It doesn't matter whether you are a lion or a gazelle. When the sun comes up, you'd better be up and running!

If you are serious about achieving something meaningful in your life, take the first step. Starting tomorrow, wake up one hour earlier than usual, it will give you an extra 365 productive hours in a year. That's like getting nine extra weeks at work. You could read a book, work on your fitness, or spend time by yourself or with a loved one. What difference would that make to your career, your health, your life?

The benefits of joining the Early Risers Club are many. And it's not only about the extra time you create for yourself. The real power is in the message it sends out to your mind. By waking up early, you are telling yourself that you are serious about achieving your goals and are willing to pay the price. You have both the physical energy and the mental strength to chase your dreams. The discipline and the willpower that help you get up early will also help you achieve a lot else in life.

When the alarm rings each morning, do you find your arm stretching out to hit the snooze button? You probably justify it by telling yourself 'just ten minutes more . . .' That's the loser's mindset, the comfort zone. If you value the comfort of the bed more than the opportunity to get ahead, don't complain when you get left behind. When the alarm rings, it's actually opportunity that's knocking at your door. And by not getting up, you are telling it to come later. Opportunity seldom knocks twice.

Do I hear you say that you know it's a good habit but

you just can't wake up early? Relax. Here's a simple 30-day plan to help you get up early, every morning. Set the alarm clock to ring 15 minutes before your regular wake-up hour. If you usually get up at, say 7 a.m., set it for 6.45 a.m. Fifteen minutes won't really make any difference. Keep the alarm clock out of arm's reach. So when it rings, you can't hit the snooze button.

Every ten days, advance the alarm by another 15 minutes, until you get to your target wake-up time. And every day, jump out of bed when the alarm rings. In 30 days, you will be getting up at 6 a.m. After a while, you will probably find that you don't need the alarm clock at all!

Has it ever happened to you that you are so excited about something which is about to happen the next day that you can hardly sleep? You seem to jump out of bed well before the alarm goes off because of the excitement and the sense of anticipation. That's what goals can do for you. Leaders are like that. They are always thinking about their goals and they are excited about getting to work on them every morning. They can hardly wait to get started!

Remember, your ability to wake up early is not a function of what time you go to bed or how much sleep your body needs. It depends only on your mind. On your commitment to your own success. To achieve something in this lifetime, get up early. Make that a habit for the rest of your life.

After all, you can always catch up on your sleep when you are dead!

If there was one single habit that could make a huge impact on your life, it would have to be this. Wake up early!

By waking up early, you are telling yourself that you are serious about achieving your goals and are willing to pay the price.

The Power of Hope

W. Mitchell is a remarkable man with an incredible story. A story that underlines the importance of a vital ingredient no leader can do without. Hope.

As a 28-year-old, Mitchell was riding a motorcycle on a highway one day when disaster struck. His motorcycle crashed into a stationary truck. His hands and hips were crushed. The petrol in the tank of his bike spilled and caught fire, and Mitchell's body was in flames. His face was charred beyond recognition. His body was covered with third-degree burns, and doctors at the hospital didn't think he'd survive. After sixteen skin grafts and numerous surgeries, Mitchell survived. With a badly scarred face and no fingers on his hands.

Six months later, Mitchell was back on his feet, making a new life for himself. He founded a company that became so successful, it made him a millionaire. He then became the mayor of his town. And despite having no fingers on his hands, he trained and became a pilot. Life was good once again.

Disaster struck again four years later: a small plane he was piloting crash-landed. The accident left twelve vertebrae crushed in Mitchell's back; his spinal cord was damaged beyond repair. He would never walk again. Consigned to a wheelchair, and with no hands, Mitchell remained unfazed and continued to lead a full life—running a large enterprise, sky-diving and motivating people around the world. 'Before my accidents, there were ten thousand things I could do,' says Mitchell. 'I could have spent the rest of my life focusing on the one thousand that I could not now do, but I chose instead to focus on the nine thousand things I could still do!' Mitchell lost his fingers, his spinal cord and the ability to walk. But he never lost hope.

If you look at the stories of successful people, you'll see familiar ingredients: big dreams, adversity, hard work, persistence, passion, discipline, failure, perseverance, more hard work and, finally, success. While the proportions may vary, the common thread holding them all together is hope. Hope is what ensures that people keep going when all seems lost. Hope is the cornerstone of all actions and achievements. And hope is what a leader instils in his team when the shoulders start to droop and spirits threaten to flag.

A student with no hope of passing an exam won't study. 'Why bother,' he'll probably tell himself, 'when I am going to fail anyway.' An overweight person with no hope of becoming slim won't go on a diet. 'Why bother? I am going to be fat anyway.' Hope is the fuel that keeps the engine of life running at all times. When the whole world seems to say, 'Give up, you can't do it', hope is that little voice inside us which urges, 'Come on, give it one more shot, you can do it.' But hope alone is never enough. You need to take responsibility. And you need to take action.

There's a little poem that's been mounted on my desk for many, many years now. The author is unknown, but it's a poem that Brian Tracy—the author and motivational guru—loves to share. The poem has given me strength and inspiration and I thought you would enjoy reading it too. Here it is:

When things go wrong as they sometimes will
When the road you're trudging seems all uphill.
When funds are low and the debts are high,
And you want to smile, but you have to sigh.
When care is pressing you down a bit,
Rest, if you must, but don't you quit.
Life is queer with its twists and turns
As everyone of us sometimes learns.
And many a failure turns about
When he might have won had he stuck it out:

Don't give up though the pace seems slow—
You may succeed with another blow.

Success is failure turned inside out—
The silver tint of the clouds of doubt.
And you never can tell how close you are.
It may be near when it seems so far:
So stick to the fight when you're hardest hit
It's when things seem worst that you must not quit.

Great leaders never lose hope. They remain optimists and recognize that their state of mind is contagious. If they have hope, so does their team. If they give up, well, so does their team.

Hope is a theme that resonates in what is described as the greatest cricket match ever played: the one-day international match between South Africa and Australia in Johannesburg in March 2006.

At the time, the record for the highest score in a 50-over game was held by Sri Lanka. In 1996, they had scored 396 for 5 versus the minnows—Kenya. Interestingly enough, three teams had scored more than 390 but no team had managed to go beyond 400! It was believed that 400 was that invisible barrier—a barrier no team could break!

On 12 March 2006, in the fifth one-day international between South Africa and Australia, history was made. Batting first, Australia did what had been seen as unthinkable—and what no team had ever done until then. They went past the 400-run barrier and posted a total of 434 for 4. The 'unbreakable' barrier was finally broken.

And guess what happened next? In reply, South Africa made 438 for 9—and won that game. Clearly, once Australia had broken the mental barrier that no team could score over 400, it was easy for South Africa to do it too. A record that had stood for ten years was broken—twice on the same day. And that's not all. Sri Lanka broke the barrier three months later. South Africa did it again. Suddenly, almost magically, the barrier was gone. In fact, since that record-breaking day in Johannesburg, the 400-run barrier has been breached six times already.

It all boils down to belief. Once you believe something is possible, the rest becomes easy. Belief is the vital first step towards achievement.

And here's an interesting sidelight to that Australia–South Africa game. When the South Africans returned for the break after being mauled by the Aussies, there was defeat written all over their faces. Their body language suggested they knew that only one result was possible in the game. They had, after all, just conceded the highest score ever in a one-day game. The spectators and experts similarly believed that Australia had the game in their pocket. Everyone believed that. Bar one. The South African captain, Graeme Smith.

When he led his team back into the dressing room, there was a stunned silence inside. And then, Smith said to his team: 'I think they are ten runs short!' That was it. That statement of the leader meant he still had hope that they could do it. The South Africans suddenly believed that if Australia could do it, they could too.

When you find your team down in the dumps, when morales around you are low, remind yourself and your team about the incredible story of W. Mitchell or Graeme Smith's 'ten runs short' quip.

Keep hope alive. Take charge. Take action. And keep winning.

Hope is what ensures we keep going when all seems lost. Hope is the cornerstone of all actions and achievements. But hope alone is never enough. You need to take responsibility. And you need to take action.

The Boy Who Swapped His Marbles

Do you find it difficult to trust other people? Do you often feel the world is out to con you? Maybe you should hear the story of the boy and his marbles. It's a simple story about two children—with a message for all grown-ups.

A little boy and girl were playing in a park. The boy had a pocketful of marbles, while the girl had some candy. As the boy kept playing with the marbles, he constantly eyed the candy in the girl's hands. His mouth was watering. He made her an offer. He would give her all his marbles in exchange for the candy. The girl agreed.

The boy slyly hid the biggest and most beautiful marble in his pocket and gave the rest to the girl. The girl gave him all the candy as promised.

That night, the girl played for a while with the marbles before going to bed. And she slept soundly.

The boy, however, just couldn't sleep. He kept wondering if the girl had hidden the best candy and kept it with her—just as he had done with his marbles.

She slept well. He didn't.

Sounds familiar? Too often our anxieties and fears are born directly of our own actions. We distrust other people and suspect them of doing things that often mirror our own actions.

When you encounter a trust issue, it is tempting to believe that the problem is with the other person. Often, the problem lies in us, not them. The way we see the world treating us is usually a reflection of the way we treat other people.

Maybe you should ask yourself if you are the one hiding the marble. As the little boy probably would have learned, owning the best marble isn't worth much if it means having to spend sleepless nights over it.

The next time you find yourself doing a candy-for-marbles swap, remember to play fair. Keep your word. Give. You might think you've got a little less in the bargain than what you could have. But you know what? You'll sleep well.

When you encounter a trust issue, it is tempting to believe that the problem is with the other person. Often, the problem lies in us, not them. The way we see the world treating us is usually a reflection of the way we treat other people.

The Elevator Not Taken!

It happens to me almost every day. The dilemma of choice. I wonder if you too have a similar tale to tell.

As I park my car in the basement and wait for the elevator to take me to my office on the sixth floor, I am confronted by a choice between two elevators. One is a 'slow' option—it stops on every floor—while the other is the 'express' option—it stops only on even-numbered floors. Which elevator should I take? The express or whichever comes first? And as I wait with the others for the elevator, it's fascinating to watch the dilemma play out every morning.

I don't know if my mind is playing tricks on me but it feels like the 'slow' elevator almost always presents itself first. We get into it rather reluctantly, longingly eyeing the panel of the elusive 'express' elevator. And as the 'slow' elevator gently lifts off, only to stop quickly on the first floor, you can hear a collective sigh of disappointment. People turn their wrists to look at that watch—'Argh! Late again!' Furtive glances at each other indicate a shared sense of dismay. If elevators had a mood indicator, this one would clearly show 'irritated'.

This sets me thinking. Our experience with elevators is probably true of our lives too. We see two paths ahead of us and are never sure which one to choose. We make a choice and then worry about the road not taken.

And often our choice is dictated not by what we know is the better option, but by what presents itself first. A bird in hand seems worth several in the bush. We are not willing to wait. So we just take the elevator that comes first. Or the first job we are offered. Waiting seems like such a waste of time.

So what's the way out? Just decide what is best, what it is that you want, and don't get distracted by other options that might lure you along the way. Allow your choices in life to be dictated by what you want to achieve and not the sequence in which those options appear before you. If it is the 'express' elevator you've decided to take, don't get tempted when life's 'slow' elevator comes up first.

But here's another thought.

Maybe we should all just learn to relax a bit and not get too stressed by every choice we need to make. Both the elevators eventually get us to the floor of our choice, to our destination—and that's what should really matter. No one's going to look at you and say, 'Ha, ha, he took the "slow" elevator!' And by not getting too caught up in the choice of the elevator, we might learn to enjoy the ride just a bit more. And maybe, just maybe, that might help wipe out the frowns on our faces and replace them with smiles. Now that's priceless!

In life, as with the elevator, it might help us to let go of our fascination with this misplaced sense of urgency. Getting there faster—nay, first—doesn't need to become an overriding tenet of our lives. Think about it. Wherever you go, you see people agitated about getting ahead. Look at the queues in the supermarket, and you'll see young couples splitting up and waiting in two separate queues—just in case Murphy is proved right again. Why give up the pleasure of each other's company for five minutes just to possibly check out 30 seconds faster? It happens every morning at airports across the country: busy executives jump queues and jostle like schoolkids to get past security first. Worth the stress? And the stares? I doubt it!

When I mentioned to my wife the other evening my daily elevator dilemma, she didn't even look up from the book she was reading. She just said: 'Why don't you just take the stairs? That would be really good for you!'

We see two paths ahead of us and are never sure which one to choose. We make a choice and then worry about the road not taken. So what's the way out?

Allow your choices in life to be dictated by what you want to achieve and not the sequence in which those options appear before you.

Getting there faster—nay, first—doesn't need to become an overriding tenet of our lives.

The Deer's Antlers and the Tail

It happens all the time. Confronted with choices, we take the easy option.

We do what's convenient rather than what's required. We float, allowing ourselves to get carried away without getting anywhere, rather than pushing ourselves and swimming to the intended shore.

Life is like that. Constantly tempting us with comfortable—but unproductive—options, luring us away from the hard work required to achieve our goals. And when you find that happening to you, do think of the two Spanish friends who went deer hunting.

They set out in their mini-truck and headed off to the jungle. Parking it at a distance, they walked into the bushes to a position of vantage down in the valley, waiting for their prey. They finally managed to shoot a deer. They then began the long journey back to their truck, dead deer in tow.

The two friends clasped the deer's tail and began to drag it towards their pick-up truck. A farmer saw them struggling and shouted out some advice: 'That's not the way to do it, fellas! God made handles for you to drag the deer. You see the antlers on the deer? Those horn-like things? Hold them—and pull the deer!'

The two friends looked at each other and decided to heed the advice. They went to the other side, grabbed the deer's antlers and continued to drag it.

Ten minutes later, one of them said, 'Boy, the farmer was right. It's so much easier this way!' 'That's right,' said his friend. 'Only problem is, we're now going farther and farther away from our truck!'

If you think about it, we are all like that. We are constantly looking for the handles—the antlers—to make our lives easier. And we start pulling as soon as we find them, forgetting that we may be headed in the wrong direction.

Clearly, it's important to ensure that in the moment of convenience, we don't lose sight of our real destination, our true goals.

We see the deer's antlers tempting us throughout our lives. A young mother sees her little one sucking his thumb. She knows it's not good for his health but prefers to ignore it. 'At least he's not crying when he's doing that!' she reasons.

A young student chooses a course of study because the institute is next door or offers convenient timings. Not because it matches her aptitude or her aspirations.

And as the film *3 Idiots* showed beautifully, some students study engineering merely because they manage to get admission into a premier institute of technology, not because they want to become engineers. Find antlers. Pull. Never mind where to!

Reflect on your own life. You will probably see several instances where you grabbed the antlers as soon as you saw them—only to find yourself moving farther and farther away from your goals. If you ask yourself why you did something, the answer will probably be 'because it was there'. In life, as in driving, it's not enough to find the best roads and then drive on them. It's important to ensure that the roads will take you where you need to go.

And as luck would have it, the path to your goals in life is often strewn with obstacles. It's a bumpy ride. There may be roadblocks and hardships. But it's often the only way to get to your goals. There will be exits, tempting you to get off the chosen path and take another road. Don't succumb to the temptation. The nice easy road may look tempting, but will it take you where you want to go?

Learning to spot the antlers to pull the deer is important. Remembering where you need to go, even more so.

In life, as in driving, it's not enough to find the best roads and then drive on them. It's important to ensure that the roads will take you where you need to go.

Put the Glass Down!

One day, a chemistry professor decided to teach his students an unusual lesson. Holding a glass of water in his hand, he asked the students, 'How much do you think this glass of water weighs?'

'About 500 grams!' came a voice from the back. 'Six hundred,' said another student.

'I don't really know!' said the professor, holding the glass up to make sure everyone could see it. 'And unless we weigh it, we won't know.'

With the glass still in his outstretched hand, the professor continued, 'What will happen if I hold it like this for a few minutes?'

'Nothing!' came the reply.

'Right, and if I hold it like this for an hour, what might happen?'

'Your hand will begin to hurt,' said a student.

'Indeed. And what would happen if I held the glass in my hand like this for twenty-four hours?'

'You will be in tremendous pain,' said one student.

'Your hand will probably go numb,' said another.

'Your arm will be paralysed and we'll need to rush you to the hospital!' said a student on the last bench.

'True,' said the professor. 'But notice that through all this, the weight of the glass did not change. What then causes the pain?'

The class went quiet. They seemed puzzled.

'What should I do to avoid the pain?' asked the professor.

'Put the glass down!' said a student.

'Well said!' exclaimed the professor. 'And that's a lesson I want you to remember. The problems and worries in life are like this glass of water. Think about them for a while and nothing happens. But think about it a bit longer and they begin to hurt. And if you think about them all day long, you will feel paralysed—incapable of doing anything. It's important to remember to let go of your problems. Remember to put the glass down!' We may not have been in the classroom that day, but it's a lesson we would all do well to remember.

It's not just problems and worries. Sometimes, we feel hurt and betrayed by a friend. And we carry that grudge throughout our lives. It grows and causes us anguish and pain. If you learn to forgive and forget, it is not only good for the people who hurt you, but is also great for you! It is the same with our fears. A failure or an incident in early childhood becomes a deeply entrenched fear over time. Fear of public speaking, or math, or rejection. You name it, and chances are, we have it. Someone gave us that glass to hold when we were kids, saying to us, 'You are clumsy, you are no good, you can't do it,' and we have faithfully held on to it all our lives. 'I can't' becomes a thought that stays in our mind and grows, inducing in us complete paralysis. Time to put the glass down!

There was once a hard-working man who lived a contented life with his wife and children. Every evening when he returned from work, he'd follow a ritual. Outside the door to his house were three nails. On the first one, he'd put his hat. On the second, he'd hang his coat. And on the third nail, he'd unwrap an imaginary turban from his head and 'put' it there. A friend happened to see this and asked what he put on the third nail every day.

'Those are my problems, my worries and my anger,' said the man. 'I have lots of that at work, but when I come home, I remember to take it off—and leave them outside. I don't take them home with me.'

Maybe you too should learn to do that. Starting today. Put the glass down. And see the difference!

We don't always realize it, but happiness is at hand!

Let go of your problems. Don't carry that grudge. Remember to put the glass down!

One 500-Rupee Note. And Two Lessons!

It happened some years ago but I can recall the evening as if it had transpired just last week. I was in an audience listening to a motivational guru. The speaker whipped out his wallet and pulled out a 500-rupee note. Holding it up, he asked, 'Who wants this 500-rupee note?'

Many hands went up. Including mine. A slow chorus began to build as people shouted, 'Me!' 'Me!' I began to wonder who the lucky one would be to whom the speaker would choose to give away the money. I also secretly wondered—and I am sure others did too—why would he simply give away 500 rupees?

Even as the shouts of 'I want it' grew louder, I noticed a young woman running down the aisle. She ran on to the stage, went up to the speaker and grabbed the note in his hand. 'Well done, young lady,' said the speaker into the microphone. 'Most of us just wait for good things to happen. That's of no use. You've got to make things happen.' The speaker's words have stayed with me ever since.

Our lives are like that. We all see opportunities around us. We all want the good things. But the problem is we don't take action. We all want the 500-rupee notes on offer. But we don't make the move. We look at them longingly and wonder who the lucky one will be—instead of making our own luck. To be fair, some of us do think of running on to the stage and grabbing the 500-rupee note. But we quickly hold ourselves back, because we worry about what people might think.

Has it ever happened that you see a successful new product or a flourishing new business and remind yourself of how you had thought of that very same idea many years ago? Well, that's not worth much. You may have had the idea first, but someone else did something about it, so he'll reap the rewards. The next time you have an idea, remember that simply thinking about doing something is of no use. Go and do something about it. The next time you see an opportunity, think of the lady and the 500-rupee note. Don't worry about what other people might think. Take action.

*

Several years later, it was another day, another time and another motivational guru. As I watched him pull out a 500-rupee note and hold it up for all to see, I thought I knew what he was going to do next. But he just asked a simple question. 'How much is this worth?'

'Five hundred rupees!' the crowd yelled in unison. 'Right,' said the speaker. He then crumpled the note into a ball and asked, 'How much is it worth now?'

'Five hundred rupees!' screamed the audience.

Next, he threw the note on the ground and stamped all over it. Then he picked it up and asked one more time, 'And how much is it worth now?'

'Five hundred rupees!' was the response.

'I want you to remember this,' said the speaker. 'Just because someone crumples it or stamps on it, the value of the note does not diminish. We should all be like the 500-rupee note. In our lives, there will be times when we feel crushed, stamped on, beaten. But never let your self-worth diminish. Remember you are still the terrific person you were. Just because someone chooses to crush you—that doesn't change your worth one bit! Don't allow your self-worth to diminish because someone says something nasty or plays a dirty trick on you.'

*

Opportunities abound but you need to take action to realize those opportunities. Don't let the words and actions of other people diminish your self-worth. Remember that, and maybe you will get all the happiness and all the 500-rupee notes that you always wanted!

Most of us just wait for good things to happen. That's of no use. You've got to make things happen.

And there will be times when we feel crushed, stamped on, beaten. But never let that diminish your self-worth. Remember you are still the terrific person you were. Just because someone chooses to crush you—that doesn't change your worth one bit!

'Never Give Up. Never, Never Give Up!'

It was the 1870s. Somewhere in a workshop in New Jersey, Thomas Alva Edison was burning the midnight oil trying to invent the light bulb.

He tried numerous experiments—all without success. He just couldn't get it right. His failures became the talk of the town and the story goes that after he had failed for the five hundredth time, a journalist interviewed him and asked, 'Mr Edison, how does it feel to have failed five hundred times? Why don't you just give up?'

'No, no, young lady,' replied Edison. 'I haven't failed five hundred times. I have just discovered five hundred ways it won't work. I am so much closer now to finding a way that will work!'

Sure enough, in 1879, Edison invented the filament light bulb, an invention that changed the world. By the time he died, the man who had failed five hundred times had got 1024 patents to his credit, and founded the iconic General Electric Company. But Edison's real contribution to mankind went beyond all this. He showed us the power of perseverance, the virtue of learning from failures and the magic of never giving up.

To succeed, one must learn to embrace failure and not be scared by it. There is a story often told about Thomas J. Watson, IBM's founder-chairman. A senior vice-president at IBM had championed an initiative that bombed—and cost the company over 10 million dollars. He was called in to meet with Thomas Watson. Fearing the worst, the vice-president walked in with his resignation letter in hand and handed it over to the boss, apologizing for the failure and the resultant loss to the company. Thomas Watson famously refused to accept his resignation saying, 'There's no way we are going to lose you. We've just invested 10 million dollars in educating you!'

Failure holds valuable lessons for us—if only we are willing to learn. Very often, we do all the hard work but when we don't see the desired results, we turn around and walk away—even though we may have been just one step away from success. The problem is, we seldom realize that we are so close to achieving our goals. On the highway of life, there are no milestones telling us that success is 1 kilometre ahead. Jacob Riis, a photographer-cum-journalist summed it up well when he said, 'When nothing seems to work, I go and look at a stonecutter hammering away at his rock perhaps a hundred times without so much as a crack showing in it. Yet at the hundred and first blow it will split in two, and I know it was not that blow that did it, but all those which had gone before.'

The option of turning away and starting a new journey is tempting because, in our minds, it takes away the stigma of failure. When you are not doing well in your job, what seems like the easiest thing to do? Quit and find another one! When you are banging away at the stone and it doesn't crack, what do you do? Try another stone. And then another. Result? Lots of effort with zero result.

Observe babies who are learning to walk. They try and take a few steps, they stumble and fall. Then they stand up and try again. And bang, they fall again. They don't feel embarrassed. They just get up and try again, until, bingo, they can walk! If little children were like us grown-ups and gave up after a few failed attempts, we would never have learned to walk. Yet as adults, we forget that lesson. We are scared to take the first steps, because we are scared we might fail. And the first time we taste failure, we give up.

A group of schoolchildren once asked Sir Winston Churchill what he thought was the secret of success. Churchill's response? Just seven words: 'Never give up. Never, never give up!'

Winners never quit and quitters never win.

Thomas J. Watson offered valuable advice to his vice-president that day. It's advice that holds good to this day for all of us: 'If you want to succeed, double your rate of failure.' Don't dwell on your lack of success. Don't play the blame game. Don't doubt your ability. Learn from your mistakes. Refocus on your goals. And keep going.

So adopt the Edison mindset. Fail often, but never lose sight of your goals. Sooner or later, there is bound to be light.

Failure holds valuable lessons—if only we are willing to learn. Very often, we do all the hard work but when we don't see the desired results, we turn around and walk away—even though we may have been just one step away from success. The problem is, we seldom realize that we are so close to achieving our goals.

Nelson Mandela and the Fine Art of Forgiving

10 May 1994 was a very special day for South Africa. It was a day that witnessed an event which not too many people had thought would come to pass. It was the day when Nelson Mandela became the first democratically elected President of South Africa. It was a day of transition—from an era of apartheid and injustice to a new dawn of freedom and democracy.

But there was something else that happened the same day, which was quite remarkable. Nelson Mandela showed a trait that was to mark him out as a terrific leader. Here he was, emerging after spending twenty-seven long years in jail. Most people thought that he would come forth with a thirst for revenge, a burning desire to settle scores with the people who may have wronged him and kept him in jail. Mandela instead did something else. In a gesture that sent a message to the world at large, he invited his former jailers to attend his presidential inauguration—as VIP guests! Three men who had held the keys to his prison cell were special invitees on that momentous day!

Mandela knew that in his journey towards rebuilding the nation, what was needed was not revenge and retribution, but reconciliation. Revenge is linked to the past. Reconciliation is what paves the way for a better future.

People had feared that the transition in South Africa could mean the start of a bloodbath as the oppressed blacks might seek revenge against the whites. This would have put South Africa back on a one-way street to destruction. But with that one act, Mandela made it clear that his nation's future—its development and success—would lie in forgiveness, not hatred.

Revenge and vendetta may make for great themes in movies, but in life, they don't serve any purpose. Learning to forgive is a skill that we must all embrace. Carrying a grudge in life only makes you overweight—and in turn slows down your progress. Shed that excess baggage. Shun that desire to settle scores. Revenge is a lose-lose proposition that can distract you from the path to prosperity.

Learning to forgive and forget can also help ensure that you don't burn your bridges. You've probably heard of people who parted ways with their bosses or friends in a rather messy fashion only to regret it when their paths crossed again. You never know whom you will meet and, more importantly, whom you will need on the road ahead. Making enemies can seem like a momentary stress reliever, but it usually serves no purpose and comes back to haunt you later in life. Friendships and partnerships get broken over petty issues that balloon into irreconcilable differences. Don't nurture that hatred. Don't carry that grudge. Learn to forgive.

The magazine *Fast Company* once carried a story of a guy called Pat Keeley, who started up a small company called PSS in the United States. Like all start-ups, it had its early struggles with funding the business. The company raised debt from a bank in Florida and business kept growing—a tad too fast perhaps. As a result the company kept exceeding its lines of credit. And that prompted the nervous bank to recall the loan. That made Pat extremely angry with the bank. He felt done in, and the company was forced to raise equity from employees to tide over what he perceived to be a bank-made crisis.

Some years later, the bank managed to lure PSS back with a fresh loan. Despite the anger over the earlier treatment meted out to them, Pat agreed to restart a relationship with the bank. After all, PSS needed the money! But as luck would have it, the past seemed to be replaying itself one more time, and the relationship between the bank and the company deteriorated once again. And once again, the bank recalled the loan.

Pat was furious. How could they do it? That's when

Pat swore to his staff: 'We are going to bury the bank!' He ordered a casket and put all the loan papers and correspondence in it, got a tombstone made and invited his colleagues at PSS for the funeral. As they gathered in the office backyard, one colleague said 'Hey Pat! It's a glorious day! Why don't we get on your boat and have a burial at sea?'

'No way will I do that!' replied Pat. 'You never know when I would have to dig up that casket and kiss the bank's ass again!'

The next time you have an argument, disagreement or fight, don't push yourself into a corner from where there's no coming back. Keep the door open. Don't drop the casket into the sea!

Remember, Mandela forgave the jailers who were responsible for his twenty-seven-year ordeal. Is it that difficult for us to forgive a colleague or a friend or a business associate for causing us a little temporary grief?

Learn to forgive. Carrying a grudge in life only makes you overweight—and in turn slows down your progress.

Lessons from Burger University!

What's common to Amazon.com founder Jeff Bezos, American comedian Jay Leno and McDonald's Corporation CEO Jim Skinner?

They all started their careers working at a McDonald's restaurant! And they are just a few of the several successful, rich and famous folks who flipped burgers at McDonald's outlets. If you are a young individual about to start work, you might learn some valuable lessons from the people whose first job was at McDonald's. Lessons which could help you succeed in any career you choose to pursue.

1. No job is too small. Many young people keep waiting for the 'right job' to come along. The jobs they get are, in their opinion, either too lowly or not well paid enough. So they continue to wait in vain. Several successful people chose to take on the rather ordinary job at a Mac outlet. It worked wonders for their careers. Don't wait. Take the work you get—and get to work!

2. Boring is normal. Working in a burger restaurant can

be boring and monotonous. This is probably true of many workplaces out there. Young people get bored easily and seek change almost too soon. Long-term success requires the ability to stay disciplined, and to keep performing a task day in and day out. Jeff Bezos recalls having to crack three hundred eggs a day at McDonald's. Doing that right probably helped him ensure that Amazon.com gets it right across millions of transactions every day! The ability to stick it out and persevere is priceless.

3. The customer is always right. Never mind what role you play—and how high you rise in the hierarchy, you will find that you need to serve customers and look after them well. The customer could be internal—within your organization—or external. Many people allow their egos to come in the way of their serving other people. Starting off in a sales role—or in a fast food joint—is a good way to put your ego in its place. And once you learn to do that, you will find that you enjoy serving, nay delighting, your customers for the rest of your life.

4. Success does not come in an instant. The road to the top is long. It takes hard work, increasing levels of responsibility and consistent performance to progress in your career. Don't expect to be rewarded for flashes of brilliance. But as it happened to Jim Skinner, three decades of doing it right and doing it well saw him rise from just another guy behind the counter to that guy in the corner room.

5. Roll up your sleeves and get your hands dirty. Great corporate leaders never fight shy of doing the 'small tasks'. Even today, the CEO of India's largest FMCG company will happily dust a shampoo pack lying in a store. Most heads of automotive companies enjoy getting under the car and getting some grease on their hands. These are habits that you imbibe early in your career. Jay Leno recalls a time when someone spilled a huge can of tomato ketchup on the floor of the McDonald's restaurant he was working at—and he had to help clean up the mess. If he could do it, you should too!

6. The magic of teamwork. In a fast food outlet, you quickly learn that you are only a small part of a larger team. Someone does the burgers, someone else the fries and yet another person takes the orders and the payment. Each person has a role to play in ensuring that the customer has a great experience! And they all share the pride of being on the same team. See how proudly they sport the McDonald's logo—right on their hearts!

No matter where you choose to work, remember the lessons the people learn when they start out at McDonald's.

So in case you are looking for a first job, be willing to do all that they do at a burger place. Remember, the pay may be small. But the leadership lessons you learn early in life will have a huge impact on your future career!

The ability to stick it out and persevere is priceless.

The road to the top is long. It takes hard work, increasing levels of responsibility and consistent performance to progress in your career. Don't expect to be rewarded for flashes of brilliance.

The Lincoln Lessons in Leadership

Are you one of those bright-eyed young people hoping to join the corporate world and make your mark as a leader? Your mind is probably a melting pot right now, filled with dreams of becoming a successful manager and questions about the right things to do. It is also perhaps brimming over with anxiety and fear that the dream of success could become the nightmare of failure.

If you are looking for inspiration, look no further than the sixteenth President of the United States of America, Abraham Lincoln. He didn't go to business school. In fact, he failed in his attempt at running a business. But Lincoln's life is a terrific story of never letting failure come in the way of realizing goals.

You probably know of Lincoln as a great American President. But do you know of the several failures he endured before getting there? Lincoln tried to get into law school, but failed. He borrowed money to start a business, and went bankrupt. He got fired from his job. He lost eight different elections. But none of this deterred him. He kept trying, kept doing his best. And finally, he became one of the greatest leaders the world has ever seen.

The next time you find disappointment and failure staring you in the face, think of Lincoln. In fact, think like him. His life and his words of wisdom could be excellent allies as you prepare to embark on your journey to greatness. Here are four quotes from Lincoln that are worth remembering:

1. 'I am a slow walker, but I never walk backwards.' We all tend to worry about our inadequacies. We are concerned that we are not good enough. The trick is to focus not on how good you are, but on getting better. It is a good idea to ensure that you are moving towards your goal at all times. You may make slow progress but make sure you are making progress at all times.

2. 'I will study and get ready, and perhaps my chance will come.' Someone once said that luck is what happens when preparation meets opportunity. If you sometimes feel that Lady Luck is not smiling on you, maybe it's because you are not preparing hard enough. The opportunity is there, but you aren't quite ready to grab it. Don't let that happen. Work hard. Your time will come.

3. 'Whatever you are, be a good one.' Your dream must not merely focus on becoming something—but on being good at whatever you choose to do. Whether you are a salesman or a software programmer, be a good one! Too often, we spend all our waking hours dreaming of being someone else or doing something else. Whatever you do, do it well.

4. 'I do not think much of a man who is not wiser today than he was yesterday.' Learning is never-ending. Stay focused on learning new skills, new tricks. You probably are busy poring over word lists and learning the meanings of new words as you prepare for an entrance exam. The exam will come and go, but the habit should stay forever. Remain curious about learning new words and expanding your vocabulary. It's not about the words—it's about the habit of learning.

There are two other aspects of Lincoln's persona that marked him out as an outstanding leader. The first was his remarkable ability to put together the best possible team to work with him. People who fought bitterly against him in an election and were defeated, were soon wooed by Lincoln to join his team. No bitterness, no hang-ups and absolutely no animosity. Just a desire to harness the best minds to give himself the best possible chance of success! Across corporate boardrooms around the world, we see two contenders for the top job. When one of them gets it, the other usually leaves the organization. And with him goes all the experience and knowledge that had made him a strong contender in the first place. If only more leaders took a leaf out of Lincoln's book—and made sure they retained their rivals—to ensure they had the strongest team at their disposal.

Finally, here's a little story that sums up the great man. One morning, Lincoln was readying himself for another day in the office when a senior official walked into his house. He was surprised to see the President of America polishing his shoes. 'What, Mr President, you polish your own shoes?' exclaimed the official.

'Yes,' said Lincoln, barely looking up. 'Why, whose shoes do you polish?'

Retain your humility. Don't let titles and success go to your head. Do those little tasks that remind you that you are just another human being. Don't fall into the trap of believing you are greater than everyone else merely because you have a fancy degree or a big-sounding title. Remember to polish your own shoes!

As you journey forward, do remember the Lincoln lessons. They'll help you. Not just in the tests you face in your career but also in the larger examination called life!

Retain your humility. Don't let titles and success go to your head. Do those little tasks that remind you that you are just another human being. Remember to polish your own shoes!

Keep Your Cool. Be Careful What You Say

Have you heard the story of the bright little kid who was prone to losing his temper? He would end up saying harsh words to his friends and family without realizing the impact of his angry outbursts.

Intent on mending his son's ways, his dad decided on a plan. He gave his son a sack of nails and told him that every time he lost his temper, he must hammer a nail into the wooden fence at the back of their farm. The son agreed. The first day, he hammered thirty-five nails into the fence. As the days passed, the number of nails hammered into the fence gradually decreased. It was quite a task going all the way to the back of the farm and hammering a nail. The young lad soon figured it was easier to simply control his temper.

And then, one day, he did not lose his cool at all. A day of no nails! Delighted, he told his father about it. And the father said that for every day that he did not lose his temper, he should pull out a nail from the fence. The boy did as told, and some months later, all the nails in the fence had been removed. The boy was pleased and so was his dad. He led his son to the back of the farm and pointed to the fence, saying, 'You have done well, my son, and I am proud of you. But notice the holes left behind by the nails? They will never go away. The fence will never be the same again. It's like that with our anger too. When we are angry, we say things that leave a scar. And no amount of apologizing later can ever remove those scars. Remember that!'

It's a lesson we would all do well to take to heart.

Keep your cool. Don't lose your temper. And you will see a significant improvement in your relationships. People will like you more, they will respect you a lot more, and you will find that hardly anybody gets angry with you. If you find yourself losing your cool often, maybe you should set yourself a punishment equivalent to hammering nails into the fence. Like that boy, you too might then find yourself controlling your temper a lot better. You can never really win when you get angry. Along with your temper, you end up losing a whole lot more.

More importantly, be careful what you say when you are angry. Choose your words with care. Those words can leave a permanent scar. They may be said in the heat of the moment but the damage could be permanent. And while you can apologize profusely and say sorry a million times, the damage is never completely undone. Saying 'sorry' is like using one of those erasers attached to the end of a pencil. It's easy to use, it feels like you have erased what was written, but the marks remain on the sheet of paper forever.

In this era of instant messaging and on-the-go emails, it's become even more important to watch your words. If you are upset and want to shoot off an angry email or message, hold it! Draft a mail perhaps—but leave it as a draft. Don't hit the 'send' button whilst you are still angry. Tell yourself that you will take a look at it the next morning. Chances are, with a cooler head the next morning, you will realize the folly of sending out the angry email. And it does not matter if you are in the right or think your anger is justified. If you lose your cool, you lose. Period.

So the next time you are angry and want to say something, take a deep breath. Pause. And maybe say nothing at all.

Starting today, resolve to keep your cool. Watch what you say and see the difference!

Be careful what you say when you are angry. Choose your words with care. Those words can leave a permanent scar. They may be said in the heat of the moment but the damage could be permanent. And while you can apologize profusely and say sorry a million times, the damage is never completely undone.

The Magic of Setting Goals

Imagine a game of football with a slight twist. It's Manchester United versus Chelsea. There's Van Persie and Rooney, Lampard and Terry. But there are no goalposts. What would happen?

The players would dribble and pass—but not know what to do after that. They wouldn't know in which direction to kick the ball. The defenders would have nothing to defend. And while Rooney would probably still swerve that free kick, he would have no target to hit. Soon, the players would probably lose the motivation to sweat it out and strive harder. There would be no winners, no result, no game.

Sounds silly, right?

But that's just the way many of us lead our lives. We have no clear goals. We run hard and dribble and wait for the pass. But we have no goals.

Writing down goals is the first and most significant step you can take towards achieving success in life. Goals give purpose to life. As the saying goes, if you don't know where you are going, any road will take you there.

There's an old saying that people who don't have goals are condemned to work for those who do. So never mind which side you are on right now, it's never too late to set goals.

Here is a five-step plan to help you set goals and get you started on your journey to success:

Step 1: Decide what you want. Set balanced goals. Make sure you cover all areas of your life—career, relationships, wealth, health and your interests. Too often, you can set yourself a unidimensional goal, and once you achieve that, you feel that's not quite what you were looking for.

Step 2: Make sure your goals are SMART (Specific, Measurable, Actionable, Realistic, Time-bound). So if you want to lose weight, don't just say, 'I want to weigh less'. (That's a wish, not a goal.) Make a statement: 'I will shed five kilos and weigh sixty kilos by the 31st of July.' That's SMART.

Step 3: Write them down. Just the act of putting your goals down on paper will increase your commitment to achieving those goals. A goal that's only in your mind is no goal at all.

Step 4: Commit to doing whatever it takes. One American billionaire had a simple two-step formula for success: determine exactly what you want, be willing to pay the price. Many of us have goals (losing weight, for instance) but are unwilling to pay the price (saying no to that cheesecake!). When it comes to achieving your goals, you cannot pay by your credit card. You must pay in advance, in full. Often, you will hear someone say, 'Once I get promoted, I will stay late and work hard'. No, that won't do. If you want to get promoted, start by putting in the extra effort. You cannot reap first and sow later.

Step 5: Take action. What does it take to achieve those goals? Determine the steps you need to take—and take the first step right away. It may be just one small step, but take it nonetheless. That old Chinese proverb still holds true: A journey of a thousand miles begins with a single step.

The importance of taking action can hardly be overstated. We all have dreams. What separates the achievers from the rest is the ability to take action.

There was once a devout man who prayed to God that he should win the jackpot. He prayed regularly, but someone else always seemed to win the weekly lottery. He prayed harder, urging the gods to reward his devotion. But the gods did not seem to be listening.

Disappointed and angered by his lack of success, he looked heavenwards and yelled, 'Why am I not winning the lottery? I've been praying regularly. That's unfair!' Suddenly there was lightning and thunder. And then a voice from above said, 'For God's sake, will you please go buy a lottery ticket first?'

Make a beginning. Today. Don't go to bed tonight until you have written down your goals. And then take that first step. Do one thing—any one thing that will take you closer to your goals.

Remember, to win the lottery, you've got to buy that ticket first!

Writing down goals is the first and most significant step you can take towards achieving success. Goals give purpose to life. There's an old saying that people who don't have goals are condemned to work for those who do. So never mind which side you are on right now, it's never too late to set goals.

If You Are Not Enjoying the Ride, Get Off the Bus!

If you find yourself stuck in a job you hate, and if wealth and fame look like distant dreams, you should hear the fascinating story of a woman called Gail Kelly.

Gail is a South African who rose to become the CEO of one of Australia's largest banks, Westpac. She is one of the wealthiest—and most respected—people in Australia today. But it wasn't always like this.

Born in 1956, Gail had an ordinary upbringing and education, culminating in a degree in arts. At twenty-one, she got married to her college sweetheart, and when his work took him away to Zimbabwe, she moved too. They returned a year later and Gail took up a job as a teacher in a government school.

All she remembers from those days is the bunch of difficult students she had to manage. She vividly recalls getting angry with a student who had left his jersey inside a sports room she had just locked up. 'I felt ashamed of myself for screaming at the little kid. I was allowing my unhappiness to affect who I was!' she recalls.

The next day, as she sat in the school bus, she wished the school didn't exist. She hated the thought of going back to the school. She decided she must do something about it. And she did.

She got off the bus.

That was the turning point in her life. She applied for and got a job as a teller in a bank. She did well and soon got promoted to a role in human resources. Some years later, at age thirty, pregnant with her first child, she enrolled for an MBA degree. After completing that, she went back to work for the same bank, and her career continued to zoom. She was soon pregnant again and was surprised to discover that she was carrying triplets. Five months after the birth of her troika, she was back at work. Back to doing what she enjoyed.

To provide for a better future for their children, Gail and her husband decided to migrate to Australia. Gail was forty-one. She went to work for a bank there. And the rest, as they say, is history.

Gail attributes her success to a lot of things: passion, hard work, the MBA degree, a supportive husband and fabulous teams. But most of all, she knows that none of this would have been possible if she had not decided to quit her teaching job and 'get off the bus' that day. Gail's story could be yours too. Even a schoolteacher can become the CEO of the country's largest bank. Just do what you enjoy, work hard and believe in yourself. Don't allow excuses (no MBA degree, need to bring up kids, moving locations) to interfere with your progress.

So what's Gail's message for her employees and for all of us? It's simple. If you are not enjoying the ride, get off the bus. There might be more fulfilling careers waiting for you.

Too many of us spend all our lives in jobs we hate. We hate every minute of it, we complain, we show our bitterness, it affects our performance and yet we don't act to change things. We lack the courage to call it quits. We hesitate to get off the bus.

There is also a flip side to this—there are many amongst us who board the wrong bus. But once inside, we start enjoying the comfortable pushback seats, the air-conditioning, the personal entertainment system and the wonderful companion in the next seat. We push away the recurring thought that we are on the wrong bus, headed to a place we do not want to go to, saying, 'Where would I find such comfortable seats? And such wonderful co-passengers?' We wonder, 'If I left this comfortable air-conditioned bus and moved to a rickety non-air-conditioned one, what would people say?' And with these thoughts we stay put on the wrong bus, going farther and farther away from our destination.

Don't let that happen to you. It is better to be on a rickety bus that's headed to the right place than to ride comfortably on the wrong bus!

If you need further inspiration, maybe you should hear about Supam Maheshwari.

Supam was a bright young lad who graduated from the prestigious Indian Institute of Management in Ahmedabad. And promptly landed what many would consider a dream job: a cushy, well-paid start with a high-profile MNC, PepsiCo.

A few months into the job, and the glitz began to wear off. As Supam sat on the Pepsi truck in Mumbai selling colas to stores on the street, he knew this wasn't quite what he wanted to do in life. The lure of working with a passionate team and fighting the cola wars was strong but Supam's dreams were pointing in a different direction. He got off the Pepsi truck.

Supam embarked on a new journey as an entrepreneur. The big fat salary was suddenly gone. When curious relatives and well-wishers asked what he did for a living, his family could no longer proudly proclaim he worked for PepsiCo. But Supam discovered joy in slogging it out as he and a bunch of friends set up Brainvisa. It became a well-respected e-learning service provider. Supam built up the business and later sold it. He then started his second enterprise, FirstCry.com, which he hopes to build into Asia's largest e-commerce site for baby products. Seeing Supam smile contentedly, snuggled between diapers and toys in his 50,000-square ft godown, it's hard to imagine what might have been, had Supam not got off the Pepsi truck!

Life is too short to be wasted doing things you don't enjoy. Doing what you enjoy offers you your best chance of success. It also gives you the strength to overcome all odds.

So if you are not enjoying what you are doing, do a Gail Kelly and Supam Maheshwari. Take the first step.

Get off the bus!

If you are not enjoying the ride, get off the bus. Life is too short to be wasted doing things you don't enjoy. Doing what you enjoy offers you your best chance of success. It also gives you the strength to overcome all odds.

Hold the Door Open!

It has probably happened to you before. As you walk towards the door of an office or a hotel, the person walking in front holds the door open for you. Remember how good it made you feel—if only for that moment? The other person may have been a perfect stranger—but that one act made you feel you had a friend.

Isn't it surprising that although we all feel good when someone holds the door open for us, we seldom do the same for others? How come?

It's probably because we are all preoccupied with ourselves and obsessed with getting ahead. Here, then, is a life-changing lesson they don't teach you in any school: 'Hold the Door Open'. HTDO!

The world can be divided into two types of people. Those who push open a door, walk through and let it slam behind them. That's about 99 per cent of the population. And there's the 1 per cent who open the door and hold it open to allow the next person to walk through. Learn to do that, and you too could join the select 1 per cent club.

Holding the door open is not just an act of courtesy, it's a mindset. It says you care for people, that you are not so caught up in your own progress that you have scant regard for other folks. It shows that while you may be in a hurry, you still have time for others. It marks you out as a leader who walks faster, pushes ahead, opens doors but is then mindful of his team, checking their progress, helping them get past barriers. HTDO doesn't merely make other people feel good. It makes you feel good too.

The habit of holding the door open translates into a behaviour of helping and caring. On the night before the math exam, you help a friend who is struggling to pass instead of focusing on scoring an extra mark yourself. The friend will never forget that. At the buffet table, the HTDO habit makes you pick up a plate and offer it to the lady behind you in the queue. The smile you see on her face is quite priceless. Small gestures all, but they make a huge difference. HTDO marks you out as someone special.

Try it. Become an HTDO person. And get the habit that separates winners from losers.

I love the story of what happened to a hotshot sales manager (let's call him Vijay) on a Sunday evening in the parking lot of a shopping mall. The parking lot was packed. Cars were crawling with anxious drivers looking for that one vacant slot. And Vijay, sharp and aggressive as he was known to be, spotted a vacant space ahead and quickly zoomed in. He could see another car trying to reverse into the same slot, but Vijay was determined to beat the other man to it. And he did! Vijay felt jubilant—as we all sometimes do with life's little victories. The old man driving the other car was disappointed. He looked Vijay in the eye and continued his search for another parking slot.

Two days later, Vijay was preparing for one of the biggest moments of his career. He was close to winning a big contract for his company. And all that was left now was the formal handshake meeting with the client's CEO. As Vijay walked into the client's office and saw the CEO, he felt a sudden sense of discomfort. Yes, it was the same man from whom he had snatched the parking slot on Sunday. And you can guess what happened thereafter. Alas! If only Vijay had grown up with the HTDO habit! The habit of caring for other people!

Winning in life is less about naked ambition and more about helping other people win. As someone once said, 'It's nice to be important. But it's more important to be nice!'

Make a beginning. Hold the door open!

Holding the door open is not just an act of chivalry, it's a mindset. It says you care for people, that you are not so caught up in your own progress that you have scant regard for other folks. It marks you out as a leader who walks faster, pushes ahead, opens doors but is then mindful of his team, checking their progress, helping them get past barriers. HTDO doesn't merely make other people feel good. It makes you feel good too.

Good Enough Seldom Is!

Do you want to go somewhere but don't know the way? Simple. Just punch in your destination on your smartphone or tablet and in an instant you will get directions on how to get there. There is a plethora of apps and websites out there to help you get to wherever you want to go. Unfortunately, that's not the case for your goals in life. Those apps and websites don't offer us roadmaps to get to our goals. At least not just yet!

Most young people have identical goals. They want to be loved, healthy, happy and successful. And rich! But here's the problem. As we set off on the journey towards our goals, the path ahead of us seems to diverge into two. One looks like a fast and easy road full of shortcuts. It's the path of least resistance. And the other is a long hard road, often strewn with obstacles. No prizes for guessing—most of us take the easy way out!

Looking for shortcuts becomes a habit. We make compromises. This mindset soon engulfs our lives. We don't push ourselves to succeed; we merely set ourselves the objective of not failing. We don't play to win. We just want to avoid losing.

And so we love helpful hints such as, 'If you study these three sections, you can get thirty-five marks.' Or, 'If you attend classes twice a week, you won't be on the blacklist.' Unfortunately, this attitude pervades our life and becomes a habit. We stop striving for the greatness that we are all capable of. '*Chalta hai*' becomes our defining motto. And as someone rightly said, 'Good is the enemy of great.' The next time you are about to submit a half-cooked project report or do less than the best you can, hit the pause button. And think of the story of the sculptor.

There once lived a sculptor in a small town. He was working on a huge idol of a goddess for the local temple, when a young woman walked into his workshop. As she marvelled at his work, she noticed another idol, almost identical, lying on the ground. 'Do you need two of these?' she asked. 'No,' came the reply. 'We only need one. But the first one got damaged in the finishing stages. Hence I am doing it again.'

The young woman looked closely at the idol on the ground. It looked perfect. She could not see any signs of damage. 'Where is the flaw?' she asked. 'Look carefully,' said the sculptor, 'and you will notice a scratch under the left eye.' 'Wait a minute!' said the young woman. 'Where will this idol be installed?'

The sculptor explained that it would be installed on a fifteen-foot-high platform inside the temple. The woman quickly retorted, 'At that distance, who will know there is a scratch beneath the eye?'

The sculptor smiled, took a deep breath and said, 'I will.'

Now that's a good reminder of what excellence is all about. It comes from inside, not outside. And it's an attitude. One which we would all do well to inculcate in ourselves. Commit to doing your best at all times. Don't compromise, ever. Whatever you do, give your 100 per cent. Aim to be the best. And do that not because someone else tells you to do it—but because YOU want to.

And make sure you always, always do the right thing. Don't tell yourself, 'It's okay, no one will notice.' Remember, someone is watching all the time. And that someone is you. Your character is defined by how you behave when you know no one is looking.

If you create an idol with a scratch and think no one will notice, you will soon find another scratch appearing in your work and then another. You will spend a lot of time and effort concealing those scratches, hoping no one notices. Instead of becoming a master sculptor, you will soon become a patch-up artist. Instead of becoming a masterpiece, your life becomes just another flawed piece of work. In both cases, what makes the difference is not the skill. It's your attitude.

Across organizations, what seems to separate the truly valuable employees from the rest is their commitment to do their best—at all times. It's that salesman who spends an extra hour late into the evening trying to merchandise one more store or sell one more case. Not because someone else asks him to do it but because he wants to. It's that young manager who goes over his presentation one more time to make sure there are no typos or data inaccuracies. This commitment to excellence then becomes a habit and creates a bunch of very special people who can be depended upon to do their best at all times.

What's true for individuals holds good for teams and organizations too. The minute you start compromising and tolerating mediocrity, it becomes the new norm. And the slide begins. We must constantly strive to give our best and be recognized, not simply aim to do just enough to ensure we don't get found out.

Get the sculptor's attitude. Commit to excellence. And make your life a masterpiece.

Excellence comes from inside, not outside. It's an attitude. One which we would all do well to inculcate in ourselves. Commit to doing your best at all times. Don't compromise, ever. Whatever you do, give your 100 per cent. Aim to be the best. And do that not because someone else tells you to do it—but because YOU want to.

Get the 40 Per Cent Advantage

Some time ago, HDFC Bank ran a TV commercial advertising their speedy ATM service. It was neat. And I think there was a nice message hidden in there somewhere for all of us!

In the advertisement, a young man parks his car near the bank's ATM, watched by a suspicious-looking rogue. As the man walks in through the door to where the automated teller machine is, the bad guy makes a signal to his team to move in for the kill. Turns out he's actually a guy whose job it is to tow vehicles that are parked in 'no parking' zones. And just as they reach under the car to hook the vehicle, they hear the car honk. The man is back from the ATM! The message is clear: HDFC Bank ATMs help you withdraw cash 40 per cent faster!

Anyone who has withdrawn cash from an ATM (or parked his car in a no parking area for just two minutes!) will find the ad easy to relate to. I like it because it's built on a nifty little consumer insight, easily converted into a benefit.

What HDFC Bank does to make it happen is actually very simple. The system remembers the amount you usually withdraw, your account number and your preferred language, and stores it as 'My favourite'. And when you click on 'My favourite', you get your cash—in a flash—and off you go. The number of screens you need to work through comes down from nine to five. And hence the '40 per cent faster' advantage!

So while all bank machines remember your name when you put in your card, HDFC Bank goes a step further. It remembers the amount of cash you usually withdraw and your preferred language. And that thoughtful little extra makes for 40 per cent faster service. Simple. But effective!

I think we could all learn from HDFC Bank and get a 40 per cent advantage in our relationships with people too. Here's how. The next time you meet someone, don't just stop at getting to know his or her name. Go a step further. Find out just a bit more. Show interest in the other person—and you'll soon get to hear about her daughter's school, her favourite movie, their last holiday to that exotic island, the misplaced driver's licence, his favourite football team. Pay attention, and you'll get to hear several interesting, unique and memorable stories. Stories that will help you connect far better the next time you meet.

We all love it when a person we meet is able to recall

a small incident or a peculiar trait. It brings a smile to the face. It breaks barriers, makes you feel closer. And the other person immediately becomes a nicer person. We hand him the 40 per cent advantage!

As the following story shows, great leaders learn to do that well.

Indra Nooyi, the CEO of PepsiCo, was on a visit to India several years ago. In my first meeting with her, she noticed I had a plaster on my left arm. I explained that I had broken my hand while playing the annual cricket match between PepsiCo and KPMG. We joked about fitness levels and talked about India's passion for the game of cricket, before getting on with the business at hand.

We met several months later in Purchase, PepsiCo's headquarters near New York. (I have always thought it ironic that one of the best sales organizations in the world is headquartered in a place called *Purchase*!). Indra's opening remark? 'Good to see you again, Prakash. And I am glad you haven't been jumping around a cricket field and breaking your bones!' Hard to explain why, but that opening line has stayed with me ever since—and every time I think of Indra, that line comes back to me! What do you say after that first hello? Well, the next time you meet someone new, go beyond the name. Show interest. Listen. And find that little nugget of information that can give you a huge edge in future.

Trust me. It makes a difference. As the HDFC Bank guys were telling us, a 40 per cent difference!

When you meet someone, don't just stop at getting to know his or her name. Go a step further. Find out just a bit more. Show interest in the other person and you'll get to hear several interesting, unique and memorable stories. Stories that will help you connect far better the next time you meet.

Give Yourself an 'A'!

Sometimes a seemingly ordinary event can hold valuable life lessons for us all. Like it happened at a lunch I had with a friend some years ago. As I recall it, the food was good, and the conversation delightful. But what made the lunch unforgettable was something else altogether.

As we entered the restaurant and sat down at our table, my host reached for his wallet. He pulled out a 100-rupee note and handed it to the waiter, who accepted it with a big smile. Now it wasn't the size of the tip that surprised me. It was the timing.

For the first time, I saw someone tipping for service even before we had ordered our meal. Needless to say, we got treated like royalty that afternoon. The service was quick, the waiter seemed to be hovering around us, and the broad smile never left his face. And as we walked out after an enjoyable meal, I was left wondering: why don't we all tip before a meal?

If you think about it, the lesson goes beyond tipping. Rewarding other people—and yourself—in advance can indeed make a big difference.

So what really happened at the restaurant that day? By paying the tip upfront, my friend was telling the waiter, 'I know you'll do a terrific job of looking after us!' And the waiter was probably telling himself, 'Wow! He trusts me to look after him well. I must do all I can to live up to his expectations.' Right through the afternoon, we expected great service—and got it!

Unfortunately, most of us are brought up on a diet of conditional love and recognition. 'If you come first in class, then you'll get a wrist watch.' Since only one kid can come first, that leaves the rest of us feeling inferior, unsure about ourselves. And yes, having no idea what time it is! Now imagine what might have happened if your father had given you a watch at the start of the term, said he knew you were a bright kid, and that he expected you to do well.

You would walk around knowing that someone really smart (your father!) thinks you are bright. You'd do all you could to live up to his expectations. Would that ensure you come first in class? No, not quite. But would it make you do your best and perform to your full potential? You bet! And that's really what life is all about.

There's a prestigious college of music in the United States that attracts the brightest talent from all over the world. The teachers there faced a problem: although the students were extremely gifted, several of them were becoming nervous wrecks after entering college. The competitiveness and pressure seemed to be telling on the students. They were anxious, thinking: 'Will I finish at the bottom of my class? Am I good enough?' And the creative spark required for their musical talent to flower often got snuffed out as a result of the pressure and anxiety.

So here's what the college did. Every student was told upfront that he or she would get an 'A' at the end of the year. What the students had to do was write a letter—dated the following year—explaining why they had 'earned' the A grade; what they had learned, what they had achieved and how they had become better people. This ensured that the students were going through college with less stress—and becoming far better musicians. They were living up to their A grades!

The pressures that the students faced at the music college were no different from what most B-schoolers experience at some of the finest institutions in the country—or what we see among high-potential employees in a large organization. They are all there because they are good but the pressure to excel and the competitiveness often ignite doubts. 'Am I good enough?' becomes a recurring thought. It may be a good idea to give them an 'A' right at the outset.

This would also alter the role of the teacher and the leader. Instead of merely evaluating the employee or the student, the role changes to one of facilitating the student to get an 'A'. Most young employees would empathize with that little kid who told his schoolteacher: 'Don't just mark my paper. Help me get an A!'

Here's a good exercise to try: award yourself 'Employee of the Year' or 'Student of the Year' today. Write down all the great things that the company CEO or college principal would be saying about you at the end of the year. Do that and you'll soon find yourself doing the things you've written down! Rest assured, you'll have a terrific year!

Musicians and waiters—and you and I—we are all just the same. Tip upfront. Give yourself an 'A' today.

Rewarding other people—and yourself—in advance can indeed make a big difference.

Edison's Formula for Success

You've probably heard of the Microsoft interview and the questions they ask prospective employees there ('How would you move Mount Fuji?'). We all have our own stories to tell about weird questions at job interviews. But have you heard about how Thomas Alva Edison interviewed people who wanted to work with him? That's an interesting story there!

After the initial round of questions, if Edison came across a bright candidate, he would take him out to dinner before making up his mind on whether to hire him. The interview would continue over dinner, and when the food arrived, Edison would take a bite and remark, 'I think this needs more salt!' And then he'd watch the candidate.

If the candidate added salt before tasting the food he would not be hired. However, if the candidate tasted the food first and then decided if salt needed to be added Edison would hire him. Edison knew that people who easily believed what other people had to say, or made assumptions without first-hand knowledge or experience, would not be able to look afresh at problems and find innovative solutions. They would have closed minds, he reckoned. Edison was looking for people with a mind of their own and the conviction to back it.

We all know people whose potential and dreams remained unrealized because they did not have the conviction to back their instincts. They chose a line of study or a career simply because someone else said it was best for them. They did not chase their passion just because someone said it was doomed, it wouldn't work. In many cases, they gave up even without trying, assuming they couldn't do it—simply because someone else had said it couldn't be done. We all have had great ideas but not all of us have gone on to work on them and make them come to life. Only to discover later that someone else did exactly what we'd had in mind and found great success.

Do your own thing. Make mistakes. Live on the edge. Chase your dreams. Don't just go by what other people tell you. That may be safe but it's unlikely to get you the success you deserve.

Go for it. And yes, don't blindly add the salt!

Do your own thing. Chase your dreams. Don't just go by what other people tell you. That may be safe but it's unlikely to get you the success you deserve.

Act Selfish. Help Someone Today!

It's a story that is over a hundred years old but the lessons are still relevant today. The year was 1892. The place: Stanford University. An eighteen-year-old student was struggling to pay his fees. He was an orphan and, not knowing where to turn for money, he came up with a bright idea.

A friend and he decided to host a concert on campus to raise money for their education. They reached out to the pianist Ignacy J. Paderewski, who was quite a superstar then. Paderewski's manager demanded a guaranteed fee of 2000 dollars for the piano recital. They agreed. A deal was struck. And the boys began to work to make the concert a success.

The big day arrived. Paderewski performed at Stanford. But unfortunately, they had not managed to sell enough tickets. The total collection was only 1600 dollars.

Disappointed, they went to Paderewski and explained their plight. They gave him the entire 1600 dollars, plus a cheque for the balance 400 dollars. They promised to honour the cheque as soon as they could.

'No way!' said Paderewski. 'This is just not acceptable!' He tore up the cheque, returned the cash, and told the two boys, 'Here's the 1600 dollars. Please deduct whatever expenses you have incurred. Keep the money you need for your fees. And just give me whatever is left!' The boys were surprised and overjoyed. They thanked him profusely.

It was a small act of kindness. But it clearly marked out Paderewski as someone special. He would have been within his rights to demand his 'guaranteed money'. And why should he help two people he did not even know?

We all come across such situations in our lives. Times when other people need our help. And most of us only think, 'If I help them, what will happen to me?' The truly great people think, 'If I don't help them, what will happen to them?' Most of us think only of ourselves, the loss we might incur, the trouble we might have to go through and the sacrifice we need to make. The true greats don't think of themselves. They think of the difference their actions could make to other people. And that's what drives their actions.

They help not because someone else is watching, or because it will look good when the world finds out. They don't do it expecting something in return. They do it because they feel it's the right thing to do.

It may not surprise you to know that Paderewski went on to become the Prime Minister of Poland. He was a great leader, but unfortunately, when the World War began, Poland was ravaged. There were over one and a half million people starving in his country, and there was no money to feed them. Paderewski did not know where to turn for help.

He reached out to the United States Food and Relief Administration for help. The head there was a man called Herbert Hoover, who later became the US President. Hoover agreed to help and quickly shipped tonnes of foodgrains to feed the starving Polish people. A calamity was averted. A relieved Paderewski decided to meet Hoover and thank him in person.

When Paderewski began to express his gratitude to Hoover for his noble gesture, Hoover quickly interjected and said, 'You shouldn't be thanking me, Mr Prime Minister. You may not remember this, but several years ago, you helped two young students go through college in the US. I was one of them.'

Make it a habit to help others. It is rightly said that you can achieve everything you want in life if only you help other people achieve what they want in their lives.

Do something selfish today. Help someone! Just do it without expecting anything in return. The world is a wonderful place. What goes around usually comes around.

We all come across situations in our lives when other people need our help. And most of us only think, 'If I help them, what will happen to me?' The truly great people think, 'If I don't help them, what will happen to them?'

A Tale of Two Seas

Sitting in geography class in school several years ago, I remember how fascinated I was when we were being taught about the Dead Sea. As you probably recall, the Dead Sea is really a lake, not a sea (and as my geography teacher pointed out, if you remembered that, it would guarantee four marks in the term paper!).

It is so high in salt content that the human body can float easily in the Dead Sea. You can almost lie down and read a book! The salt content in the Dead Sea is as high as 35 per cent—almost ten times the level in normal ocean water. And all that saltiness has meant that there is no life at all in the Dead Sea. No fish. No vegetation. No sea animals. Nothing lives in the Dead Sea.

While the Dead Sea has remained etched in my memory, I don't seem to recall learning about the Sea of Galilee in geography class. So when I heard about the Sea of Galilee and the Dead Sea—and the tale of the two seas—I was intrigued.

The Sea of Galilee is just north of the Dead Sea. Both the Sea of Galilee and the Dead Sea get their water from the same source—the River Jordan. And yet, the two are very, very different.

Unlike the Dead Sea, the Sea of Galilee is resplendent with rich, colourful marine life. There are lots of plants and colourful fishes too. In fact, the Sea of Galilee is home to over twenty different types of fish.

Two seas, same region, same source of water, and yet, while one is full of life, the other is dead. How come?

Here's apparently why. The River Jordan flows into the Sea of Galilee and flows out again. The water simply passes through the Sea of Galilee—in and out—and that keeps the sea healthy and vibrant, teeming with marine life.

But the Dead Sea is so far below the mean sea level that it has no outlet. Water flows in from the Jordan, but does not flow out. There are no outlet streams. It is estimated that millions of gallons of water evaporate from the Dead Sea every day, leaving it salty, too full of minerals, unfit to support marine life.

The Dead Sea takes water from the River Jordan and holds it. It does not give. Result? No life at all.

Think about it.

As you set out on your journey in life, learn a lesson or two from the tale of the two seas. Life is not just about getting. It's also about giving. We need to be a bit like the Sea of Galilee.

We are fortunate to get wealth, knowledge, love, respect and more. But if we don't learn to give, we could end up like the Dead Sea. The love and the respect, the wealth and the knowledge could all evaporate. Just like the water in the Dead Sea.

If we develop the Dead Sea mentality of merely taking in more—more water, more money, more everything—the results can be disastrous. Make sure that in the sea of your own life, you have outlets. For love, wealth and everything else that you get in your life. Make sure you don't just get, you give too.

It's never too early to learn to give. If you give your child a hundred rupees as pocket money, encourage him to 'give' a bit. Could be a rupee, or more, but that's irrelevant. The key is learning to give and getting used to the idea.

Look around and you'll see several great leaders who are passionate teachers. They enjoy sharing their knowledge and their experiences. So don't be one of those folks who are constantly eyeing a nomination to the next executive management programme at a top B-school. Good leaders are givers. They are happy to share their knowledge, experience, time and attention.

Make sharing and giving a habit.

After all, what would you like your life to resemble? The Dead Sea—where nothing grows—or the Sea of Galilee with its colourful flora and fauna? Open the taps, unclog the outlets. And you'll open the floodgates to growth and happiness.

Life is not just about getting. It's also about giving.

Give Yourself a Friendship Medal

A telecom company's ads on TV have been telling us, '*Har ek friend zaroori hota hai* (Every friend is essential)'. As I hummed the tune the other day, my mind wandered towards friendships and I was reminded of one of my favourite stories from the Olympics. It is the story of two Japanese pole-vaulters who were also great friends. Sueo Oe and Shuhei Nishida represented Japan in the Berlin Olympics in 1936.

If you check the record books, you will see that Earle Meadows of the United States won gold in the pole vault event at the Berlin Games, clearing a height of 4.35 metres. Oe and Nishida competed fiercely for second place—but even after five hours, they remained tied. That's when the judges decided to call off the contest, leaving it to the Japanese team to decide who between the two should be given the silver!

While both of them had cleared 4.25 metres, it was decided to award the silver to Nishida since he had cleared that height in his first attempt, while Oe only cleared it on his second jump. And so the two dear friends left Berlin—one with a silver and the other with a bronze.

When they returned to Japan, they went to a jeweller and had their medals cut into two pieces. Each exchanged a piece with the other so they could stick it with the piece each of them originally had. And they both ended up owning a half bronze-half silver medal. A medal that later came to be known as the 'friendship medal'.

If you have a good friend or are in search of one, this is a story you must remember. We often find ourselves in situations where we are constantly competing—admission in a college, a job or a promotion. Often with our own friends. That's not all, we get so caught up in ourselves and the prize we are lusting after that we disregard our friends and look at them as adversaries. Friends get sacrificed at the altar of personal greed and, as we all discover later, that's a terrible deal. Don't let that happen to you. If you find yourself competing with a friend, stop and think of Nishida and Oe. And discover the joy of sharing a prize with a friend rather than beating him to it. Think of giving rather than getting. Winning a silver medal is nice. But having a half bronze-half silver medal can be even nicer!

A true friend is often the finest possession anyone can ever have. A real friend can help you find happiness and achieve all that you ever wanted. Now here's the rub. Most of us would love to have a friend like that. But the question is—are you a friend like that? Are you the person who's making a difference in someone's life?

Be the kind of person who focuses on others and is not worried only about himself. We all complain sometimes about how little our friends care for us or help us. The real question to ask is, how much do we care? How much do we help? Having a good friend is not a function of finding the right person. It's about being that right person.

We all need a friend we can trust our lives with. Imagine that you found yourself in a jail in a foreign land. And you were allowed only one phone call. Whom would you call? Who's that person you know who would do all it takes to get you out? Truth is we all need someone like that—but are not always lucky to find that friend. Is there someone out there who has your name as the person they would call if they found themselves in a foreign jail?

Get a good friend, and hold on to him or her for dear life. More important, remember to share the silver. Be the friend you'd like to have!

A true friend is often the finest possession anyone can ever have. A real friend can help you find happiness and achieve all that you ever wanted. Now here's the rub. Most of us would love to have a friend like that. But the question is—are you a friend like that? Are you the person who's making a difference in someone's life?

The Secret of Sachin Tendulkar

Sachin Tendulkar is special. And he will remain that way. Forever. Not just for the runs he has scored and the games he has won, but for the sense of pride he has instilled in an entire nation, allowing us all to believe that we can take on the world—and win. And for the sheer joy he has provided to the world at large with his masterly batting. There is no doubt about the fact that long after he has hung up his boots, he will still be spoken of as a genius, a rare talent, a superstar who lit up our galaxy.

So what made Sachin so special? Was this a case of exceptional innate talent? Those eyes that seemed to pick up a ball just a bit quicker than everyone else, those wrists that seemed to be able to turn a cricket bat into a magic wand, and the footwork that allowed him to dance down to the pitch of a ball with ballerina-like perfection—were all those just God-given gifts, lovingly bestowed on the chosen one?

Or was it his attitude? His fighting spirit and mental strength were best epitomized that day in Sialkot when, in a Test match India was fighting to save, he got hit on the nose by a bouncer from Waqar Younis. And when the non-striker, Navjyot Singh Sidhu, and the team physio advised that he retire hurt, Tendulkar dismissed their suggestion with those magical words: '*Main khelega*!' 'I'll play,' he said. Nay, he said, 'I'll fight!' Two words that defined the genius of the man!

But there's something else that might actually reveal the secret of Tendulkar's greatness. Something that goes beyond talent and attitude. Gary Kirsten, the former India team coach, spoke about it. And it's something we could all learn and benefit from.

Towards the end of Kirsten's stint as India coach, Cricinfo spoke to him about all things cricket. And of course when the discussion veered to Tendulkar and what made him special, here's what Kirsten had to say: 'Tendulkar studies the whole book for the exam! He does not leave anything to chance. He will never finish a net session till he has made sure he has done everything that he feels is required to get ready for the next match. Sometimes it means facing three hundred balls in the nets, sometimes fifteen hundred balls!'

Wow! Think about it. After twenty-five years of top-class cricket, he still studies the whole book for the exam! If he scored a hundred in a Test match, he'd probably end up facing from a hundred and fifty to two hundred balls. And yet, in practice, he could end up facing fifteen hundred balls. How many of us do that in our lives?

Several talented folks with a solid track record behind them begin to think that they can wing it past any challenge, that they don't need to prepare any more. And that sets them up for failure. Most of us grow up looking for shortcuts. What's the least effort we need to put in to get by?

But as Tendulkar showed, the truly great guys ask a different set of questions of themselves: 'What more can I do to succeed? Have I done all I can to take care of any eventuality?' Their results are driven by hard work. And not just talent or attitude. By sweat, tears and toil. Not just God-gifted talents or luck.

As we've seen before, success happens when preparation meets opportunity. The opportunity comes to us all. The question is, how prepared are we when opportunity comes knocking? Take a leaf from Tendulkar's book. Sweat it out. Prepare. Never mind how successful you are, remember, every dawn brings a new day.

We may not all have Tendulkar's talents. Or his mental strength. But we can all have his work ethic. Slog, remember to study the whole book for the exam.

Tendulkar studies the whole book for the exam! Do you?

Want to Be a Good Leader? Just Do It!

Here's a simple question to get you started. There are three monkeys sitting on a tree branch stretching out over a pond. One of the monkeys decides to jump into the pond. How many monkeys are left on the tree?

Did I hear you say, 'Two'?

Wrong. The right answer is three. You see, the monkey only made the decision to jump into the pond. He didn't actually jump! What's true for those monkeys is probably true for all of us. We take decisions and make resolutions. But for some reason, we don't follow through with action. And intent without action is really quite useless. Getting started—taking that first step—is often the master key to success. As someone once said, you don't have to be great to get started. But you sure have to get started to become great!

Great leaders have a strong bias for action—a let's-get-moving attitude that pushes the entire team to a heightened sense of activity. Do you find yourself struggling to take action on your plans and intentions?

Well, here's a five-point programme to help you move from intent to action. From good to great.

1. Make a beginning—right away. Whatever be your goal, take the first step, however small. Until you take that first step, your mind does not believe you. You need to signal to yourself that you mean business. Commit to taking action, immediately. Today. Now.

2. Break up the grand plan into smaller tasks. As the Johnnie Walker advertisement keeps reminding us, a journey of a thousand miles begins with a single step. Sometimes the task ahead looks so enormous that we feel overwhelmed and don't do anything about it. Break that up into smaller sub-tasks, and suddenly, you'll find something that's doable. Remember that old adage 'Something is better than nothing'? It still rings true.

3. Visualize your success. Think of the pleasure, not the pain. If you want to acquire an MBA degree at a premier school and plan to devote three hours a day to studying, don't think about missing the football game on television, or not being able to go out for that Saturday night bash. Think instead of the job that you could get after your MBA, the rewards that it would bring, the dreams that would get realized.

4. Create a support group. Surround yourself with people who share your objective and are co-passengers on your journey to success. The excitement of being in it together will help you fight the inertia and get you going, egged on by the rest of the gang.

5. Pay up—in advance. For most of us, monetary commitments are a strong impetus for action. The fear of losing money or wasting it can spur you into action. We follow up on our commitments, if only to ensure that our money is well spent. Plan to lose weight? Pay up for that three-month weight loss programme. Don't wait—make that commitment, financial or otherwise!

Bestselling management guru Tom Peters narrates the tale of a man who approached the legendary American financier and banker, J.P. Morgan, with an envelope and said, 'Sir, in my hand I hold a guaranteed formula for success, which I will gladly sell you for 25,000 dollars.'

'Sir,' J.P. Morgan replied, 'I do not know what is in the envelope. However, if you show me, and I like it, I give you my word as a gentleman that I will pay you what you ask.' The man agreed to the terms and handed over the envelope. J.P. Morgan opened it and pulled out a single sheet of paper. He gave it one look—a mere glance—then handed it back to the gentleman. And paid him the agreed-upon sum of 25,000 dollars!

On that sheet of paper, were written two things:

1. Every morning, write down a list of the things that need to be done that day.
2. Do them.

J.P. Morgan benefited from this advice, and you can too. Knowing what to do is often easy. We all have our to-do lists, plans and resolutions. Doing it—that's the tough bit, that's what distinguishes the truly successful from the also-rans. The Nike guys are right. Want to be a winner? Just do it!

Here's a guaranteed formula for success:

1. **Every morning, write down a list of the things that need to be done that day.**
2. **Do them.**

IV

LEADING TEAMS

'If you want one year of prosperity, grow seeds. If you want ten years of prosperity, grow trees. If you want one hundred years of prosperity, grow people.'

—Chinese proverb

Betting on Unripe Fruit

Rahul Chandawarkar is a delightful fellow. The kind of guy who can ensure that there isn't a moment of silence in what might look like a never-ending evening bash! He is an MBA who went to work for a bank, but then chose to opt out of the corporate rat race to chase his passion—journalism. He now edits a newspaper and lives in the city of his choice, Pune. In one of our early meetings, Rahul recalled his experiences from his first job and told me about his first boss. While still in college, he had started off as a rookie reporter with *Sportsworld*—the magazine that Mansur Ali Khan Pataudi used to edit.

His boss was David McMahon, the assistant editor at *Sportsworld*. And Rahul recalled with great enthusiasm the one trait that marked David out as someone rather special: his willingness to bet on youth! And here's the story:

When the Indian cricket team travelled to Pakistan in 1982–83, every newspaper sent out its most senior reporter to cover the tour. After all, this was a big tour. And whom did David choose to send? A young not-yet-out-of-his-teens lad called Mudar Patherya.

Mudar went on to do a great job, and his youthful exuberance, natural curiosity and the desire to 'live up to David's trust' ensured that *Sportsworld* had some of the finest coverage of the tour.

That a youngster will go the extra mile, do just a little bit more to prove his worth, was established on the tour to the West Indies some years later. Mudar the writer managed to pull off a scoop—as a photographer! One Sunday morning, while the senior folks were either relaxing in the hotel or sightseeing, Mudar drove out to watch young West Indian kids play beach cricket. He joined in the fun, and when his turn came to bat, he was surveying the field when he saw a familiar figure standing at slip: the big man—Viv Richards—himself. He quickly clicked a picture of the king of West Indian cricket—barechested and having a blast with the kids on the beach—with his amateur camera. The picture made it to the front page of *Anandabazar Patrika* and Mudar had another exclusive story to his credit. David's faith in the youngster had been vindicated.

Mudar went on to become one of our finest cricket writers, and now runs a successful financial communication services company with his wife in Kolkata. And I am sure he will acknowledge the role that 'early break'—that vote of confidence from David and the management of *Sportsworld*—played in his eventual success.

Mudar wasn't the only one. When it was time for Wimbledon, David, himself a terrific tennis writer, chose to pick another rookie: Rohit Brijnath. Rohit apparently did not even have a passport when he was told that he'd be covering Wimbledon! Rohit went on to become one of the best sports writers India has produced, and is also the co-author of Abhinav Bindra's acclaimed autobiography.

Most good leaders have a knack for spotting great talent. But it's the exceptional leaders who bet on that young talent ahead of its time. A big assignment, a special project or an out-of-turn promotion, and suddenly that young talent becomes hot property. Many successful people owe their meteoric rise not just to their talent, but also to that leader who was willing to bet on them. And when a leader places those bets on young talent, the whole team benefits. Notice that the story of David's greatness was narrated to me not by Mudar or Rohit, but by someone else who was on that team! And that's not all. When I shared the story with David, he gave credit for it to the publisher of *Anandabazar Patrika*, Aveek Sarkar, who had given him the early break. David was only twenty-four when Aveek Sarkar made him the assistant editor of *Sportsworld*!

The bet may not always come good. And when it goes wrong, the leader and the young prodigy often pay a price. And here's the irony: if the leader plays safe he doesn't really attract any criticism for not giving the youngster a chance. Which is why it takes a special kind of leader and a courageous one at that, to place that bet. And then the fearlessness of youth takes over. The enthusiasm and the desire to prove the leader right usually pave the way for the youngster's success.

The day after I heard the David McMahon story, India was fighting to win a Test match in Bangalore. The big hope—Sehwag—was out cheaply. And when the entire crowd at the Karnataka State Cricket Association ground roared to welcome the No. 3 batsman—local boy Rahul Dravid—they were in for a surprise. Instead of Rahul, out came the debutant Cheteshwar Pujara. Pujara had failed in the first innings and yet was now being trusted by his captain to play a defining innings. And he did. His 72-run knock helped India beat Australia. My mind went back to David and Mudar and Rohit.

Had Pujara failed, it would have been easy to say that Dhoni had erred. After all, the youngster had failed in the first innings. Why did the skipper put him under unnecessary pressure? Why change the batting order? Why . . . and the questions would have been many. Hindsight is usually pure genius.

Which is why you need to doff your hat to Dhoni, David and others like them. Bosses who bet on unripe fruit! It takes courage to bet on a youngster.

So think back. When it was your turn to take a punt on the kid, did you play safe or did you place your bets?

And hey, remember the guy who bet on you? You should probably pick up the phone and say thank you.

Clearly, our world needs more Dhonis and Davids. Make sure you add your name to that list!

Most good leaders have a knack for spotting great talent. But it's the exceptional leaders who bet on that young talent ahead of its time. It takes courage to bet on unripe fruit!

The Strong 'Why' and the Case of the Andhra Bus Drivers

As I stood sweating after a workout on the treadmill in my neighbourhood gym, I couldn't help but notice a significant change that has taken place over the years. I wondered if it's a phenomenon that's sweeping through gyms across the country. Has your gym changed too? No, I am not talking about the fitter people you see working out or the larger crowds, particularly during January, in the immediate aftermath of the New Year resolution season.

I am referring to the posters and images that typically adorn the walls of the gym. Not so long ago, all I recall seeing in the gym were large instructional posters explaining how to use the equipment. Visuals and text explaining the right moves, the correct body posture while lifting weights, how to work the bench press, and so on. There were charts showing the 20-minute fitness regimen—the series of exercises designed to cut the flab and get those fab abs. You get the drift, right?

What I was now seeing were pictures of fabulous bodies. Men and women in their training gear, lean and fit. Just the kind of bodies we all drool over and aspire to flaunt. Those six-pack abs and those wonderfully toned muscles! That's the dream that makes sure we go back to the gym even after that late night out. The how-to-get-fit stuff was gone. All you could see were the fabulous end results. The message seemed clear: if you can get people excited about wanting that fit body, they will figure out how to get there! And looking at the increasing number of people using gyms, the change seems to have worked out rather well for gym owners.

It struck me that perhaps there's a message in this for leaders too. We spend too much time explaining how to do things rather than concentrating our energies on inspiring our people with the results we want them to achieve. We focus on telling people what to do and how to do it. Instead, we should be helping them discover *why* they might want to do it. 'What's in it for me?' is still a question that tops the charts the world over.

Rather than setting an inspiring goal and getting people excited about getting there, we spend our time and energy explaining to them how to do it. It doesn't work. Not in the gym and certainly not at the workplace.

A strong 'why' trumps a set of 'hows' and 'whats' any day. Once you have a strong 'why'—a goal, a dream, a mission that you've bought into—the 'hows'—the means—are easy to find. Conversely, no matter how specific the instructions are, if you aren't excited by the goal, you are unlikely to follow those instructions. It's a bit like going on a holiday. We pick a destination we want to visit—and then look for ways to get there. You would struggle if someone gave you detailed driving instructions but you didn't know where you were going!

To quote French writer and aviator Antoine de Saint-Exupéry, 'If you want to build a ship, don't drum up the men to gather wood, divide the work, and give orders. Instead, teach them to yearn for the vast and endless sea.'

A young lad I know aspires to study at an Ivy League B-school and make a career as an investment banker. He talks passionately about wanting that Hugo Boss suit, the Hérmes tie and those Salvatore Ferragamo shoes. I am betting on his making it there!

If you are wondering whether this stuff really works, here's confirmatory evidence—from a rather unlikely source. The Andhra Pradesh Road Transport Corporation runs over 23,000 buses every day, ferrying 12 million passengers and covering 820,000 kilometres. There have been several efforts to improve the safety record of their bus service, but one particular initiative in recent times has paid off big time. From an accident rate of 0.13 per 100,000 kilometres two years ago, the accident rate has dropped now to .09. What changed?

Did the Corporation conduct more safety-related

training programmes? Did it instruct drivers to stop overspeeding? Did it improve service and maintenance? Nope. In a rather innovative move, it mandated every driver to put a photograph of his wife and children on the dashboard. That was it! Knowing someone was waiting for them to return home alive was enough to ensure that the drivers did all they could to stay safe.

Think about it and you'll realize that as leaders we spend most of our time telling people how to build the ship. Or how to increase sales and gain market share, how to reduce waste and increase productivity. Rather than getting them excited about the wonderful world beyond the shore. Or the joy of winning.

Time, then, for us to change the wallpapers in our minds. Tear down the 'how-to-do-it' messages. And replace them with vivid images of the end results. What does a winning team look like? What would being No. 1 mean to every employee? What does a Great Place To Work look like? Paint that picture. And the results will be magical—and instant.

Give your team a strong, big WHY. And the whats and hows will take care of themselves. That's true for your team. And true for you too!

Don't focus on telling people what to do and how to do it. Instead, help them discover *why* they might want to do it.

A strong 'why' trumps a set of 'hows' and 'whats' any day. Once you have a strong 'why'—a goal, a dream, a mission that you've bought into—the hows and whats are easy to find.

Two-Footed Footballers and the Corner Office

If you are a young ambitious professional hoping to climb the corporate ladder, there's a useful lesson to be learned from the world of football.

Three professors in the United Kingdom conducted a study on footballers' remuneration in Europe. Their not-so-surprising finding holds a vital lesson for us all.

Alex Bryson, Rob Simmons and Bernd Frick looked at footballers playing in the major leagues and correlated their footedness—whether they were left-footed, right-footed or two-footed—to the wages they earned. And what did they find? They discovered that two-footedness—the ability to use both feet equally well to dribble, pass and shoot—commands a significant premium! In fact, footballers who were two-footed earned, on an average, 19 per cent more than the rest. You would be hard-pressed to make a case against the two-footedness premium when there are examples like Cristiano Ronaldo, Zinedine Zidane and George Best.

For a start, two-footed footballers are a rare species. Fewer than 15 per cent of players in the leading European leagues are two-footed. Being two-footed makes them more versatile, allowing the manager or the coach to deploy them in different positions on the field. And the ability to kick the ball with either foot with equal felicity makes them dangerous players on the field.

It's the same in the corporate world. If you look closely at great leaders and successful CEOs, you'll probably see a common thread: they have two strong suits. It could be a manufacturing guy with a good feel for sales, or a marketing professional with an astute head for finance. They are people who have ensured that apart from their natural, core functional strength, they have acquired a second specialization. When hiring and promoting young talent, what most leaders look for in the candidate is that second skill—the ability with the other foot. The two-function experts find themselves in meatier roles, find greater acceptance across the organization—and make greater impact. In contrast, one-trick ponies seldom rise to the top.

As football coaches will tell you, two-footedness can be taught. So it's not as if those two-footed geniuses were necessarily 'born great'. But apparently, it's a skill that can be taught only in the early, formative years of a footballer's career. Once he is an established player, it becomes difficult to train him suddenly to become two-footed. Either you acquire the ability early enough, or not at all.

This is why all young managers should develop an interest and competence in a second function. In the early years of your career it is tempting to play to your strengths and operate in your comfort zone. Resist that temptation. Notwithstanding which function you belong to, make sure you take an interest in other facets of the business. Spend time in the factory and the market. Understand financial metrics and consumer behaviour. Remember, it has to be learned early. It's not as if you can say, 'Once I become CEO, I'll learn about the other functions'. That's usually too late.

Acquiring the power of the second foot also requires a willingness to fail, to make mistakes. As a kid playing soccer, it's tempting to get the ball on to the naturally stronger foot and play to your strengths. Developing the other foot requires a mindset that says it's okay to look silly. Those early kicks with the other foot are usually clumsy and mostly off the mark. Training that other foot is hard work, it requires practice, but ultimately it has its rewards.

Some of the better leaders and organizations recognize the incredible power of versatility and make sure that young managers are exposed to varied opportunities early in their careers. Young sales managers are assigned stints in the supply chain. The operations whiz-kid is moved into a role in human resources. Often, the first reaction of the young manager is one of apprehension. Will this slow down my career progression? Will this show up my limitations? Once they overcome these fears, most of them find the experience hugely enriching—and it stands them in good stead several years later.

If your organization is serious about building leaders, you might want to take inspiration from a little-known school in the United Kingdom. Set up in 2004 in the Scottish Highlands, it's called The Other Foot Soccer School. It concentrates solely on improving the *other* foot. The inspiration for the school was a former England player, Pat Finney, who, as you might have guessed, was two-footed. In fact, he played in all five forward positions. The school takes young kids and helps them develop strengths in 'the other foot'.

Organizations, mentors and schools would all do well to focus on developing versatility, and building multi-faceted, 'two-footed' individuals. Two-footed footballers don't just get paid more. They are rare, much sought after, and greater contributors to their team's success.

So how strong is your second suit? Time to start training 'the other foot'!

Become a two-footed player. Develop an interest and competence in a second function. In the early years of your career, resist the temptation to play to your strengths and operate in your comfort zone. Notwithstanding which function you belong to, make sure you take an interest in other facets of the business. Training that other foot is hard work, it requires practice, but ultimately it has its rewards.

The Umpire's Autograph

One of the best pieces of advice I have ever got was from an unlikely cricketing hero, many years ago. They weren't words of wisdom from a Sunny Gavaskar or a Kapil Dev. They came from a Test umpire of the1970s: a gentleman named Swaroop Kishen.

Swaroop Kishen was a star in his own right. He was a portly man who looked like the jovial Hardy from the American comedy duo of Laurel and Hardy. A lawyer by training and a wicketkeeper in his college days, he found a way to indulge his passion even while his considerable duties at the auditor-general's office kept him busy. The oversized white coat and his hard-to-miss girth made him instantly recognizable and quite lovable as well.

I have vivid memories of a Test match against Pakistan that was being played in Bangalore. There was a sudden attack by a swarm of bees. The players and the umpires threw themselves on the ground to avoid being in their line of fire. The sight of Swaroop Kishen lying on the ground—literally belly up—elicited a chuckle all around and also made it to the front pages of most newspapers the following day.

As a cricket-crazy kid growing up in Mumbai, I remember getting Swaroop Kishen's autograph during a break at a first-class game. While most fans were clamouring for the players' autographs, I was keen to get the umpire to sign in my book. And he did—prefacing his signature with three words: 'Pause and decide!' Those three words were for me not just an articulation of an umpire's philosophy, but also a pithy masterclass in effective decision-making. It has stayed in my mind ever since. Every time I need to respond to something or take a decision, the umpire's words flash into my mind—pause and decide.

Driven by impulsive responses, we often take decisions in haste. Someone says something to us—and we immediately react with words and actions that come back to haunt us later. If only we'd make it a habit to heed the late umpire's advice.

The next time you are angry or hurt, or need to make a decision, take a deep breath—before saying a word or moving a finger. The next time something goes wrong and you feel like reacting—just hold it. After the moment has passed, you will find the turmoil settling down. The mind gets clearer. And the decision that follows is usually a lot better than what you might have taken in haste.

Very often, our decisions are more like a negative vote

than a positive choice. We change jobs not because a great offer comes our way but because of one tough appraisal feedback session, or a promotion that we lost out on. We make career choices, break relationships, commit to investments—all in the heat of the moment. And the evidence we conjure up in our heads tends to be hugely biased. It's almost as if, having decided to react in a particular way, we only look at all the evidence that supports our case! In an era of increasing download speeds, we seem to be in a hurry to take decisions. In most cases, a cooler head brought about by the passage of time would have made for far better, more reasoned decisions. A thin line separates haste from speed—but it's a critical difference. Whoever said, 'Decide in haste, repent at leisure' was right. He may have said it a long time ago, but we clearly haven't learned our lesson.

There's an interesting story about a spiritual master who went on a pilgrimage with his disciples. The wise old man felt thirsty and wanted some water. A disciple quickly walked over to a nearby stream, jar in hand, to fetch some water. The stream was crystal clear and he could see the sun's rays dancing on the water. Just as he was about to fill the jar, a bullock cart crossed the stream. As the wheels churned the soil of the bed of the stream, the water turned muddy. It didn't look clean enough to drink, so the disciple went back to the master empty-handed, and explained what had happened. The master asked him to wait a while to allow the mud to settle, and then fill the jar. When the disciple went back a little while later, he was delighted to find the water was crystal clear again.

As the master took a sip of the water, he exclaimed: 'Our minds are like that stream. An external event or stimulus—like that bullock cart—can cause our minds to get muddled up. When that happens, all you need to do is relax. Just wait a while and allow the dust to settle. And the mind will be clear again.'

As I think back on the umpire's autograph, I realize that there was in fact a second lesson I learned from Swaroop Kishen. If you've ever got yourself an autograph, you will know that most cricketers—and other celebrities—hastily scribble a scrawl or a barely legible signature. It may be just another autograph for the celebrity, but for the fan, it's something to cherish for a lifetime. The umpire was different. He took the time and the effort to put in a few words before signing off. That made his autograph truly special—and it meant so much to me!

As leaders, we might be busy, but it's a good idea to ensure that when we interact with someone—even fleetingly—we give it our all. Remember, it may be just another meeting or one more letter for you, but for the colleague, it probably means a whole lot more. So if you are sitting in on a presentation, stop checking the email that's just arrived on your phone. Listen to them. You have no idea how much time they've spent preparing for this. If you are signing a piece of communication meant for a colleague—a letter of promotion or even a birthday card where the whole team signs—make it a point to personalize it with a few words. Those words won't take too much of your time—but the impact they will have on your colleague will be huge.

The next time you feel agitated or stressed and want to respond, just think of the bullock cart and the stream. And the umpire's autograph. Remember the good umpire's advice. Pause and decide!

The next time you are angry or hurt, or need to take a decision, take a deep breath—before saying a word or moving a finger. The next time something goes wrong and you feel like reacting—just hold it. After the moment has passed, you will find the turmoil settling down. The mind gets clearer. And the decision that follows is usually a lot better than what you might have taken in haste.

The Porcupine Lesson

Porcupines are fascinating creatures. It is hard to believe, but each porcupine has on average about 30,000 quills. These are really like hair but are coated with a keratin-like substance. When attacked, the porcupine responds by dashing backwards into the enemy, and several of these quills get stuck in the attacker's body causing serious injury. When one quill falls off from the porcupine's body, another quickly takes its place.

I often think there are people who take after the animal! Docile at first appearance . . . but when provoked, boy, all those quills are quickly out to get you! I didn't realize, though, that there's an interesting little story from the world of porcupines that holds a valuable—and pointed—lesson for all of us.

The story goes that it was a particularly harrowing time in porcupine land. The winter was severe and the porcupines were finding survival difficult. They were freezing to death. That's when they held a meeting to decide on a course of action. As they got together to discuss their survival strategy, they discovered that just by being in close proximity with each other they were able to feel warmer and protect each other. Being closeted together meant that their bodies generated heat which helped keep everybody warm. So they found they could survive the cold by just staying together!

But there was a problem. As they moved closer, they found each other's quills to be a bother—they poked and hurt. Feeling the discomfort, some porcupines decided to avoid the pain from the quill pokes and moved away. And as they ventured out on their own, the cold got them and they died.

Soon better sense prevailed and the porcupines realized it was better to stay together and survive rather than go out on their own and die. Getting poked by the quills of porcupines that were close to them seemed like a small price to pay for survival.

You will probably find that the porcupine story rings true in the context of our families and organizations. Often we get hurt by the words and actions of people close to us. And we move away in anger, not realizing that being away—and alone—could mean paying a bigger price. Notice how families split, siblings fight and homes break up because of small differences—the odd porcupine prick. Business partnerships and joint ventures fall apart, and employees decide to part ways—because of minor differences with their partners and colleagues. We all seem to think that going away would put an end to our troubles. No more quill pricks, we tell ourselves. But we seldom realize that going away often marks the beginning of new troubles, bigger challenges.

It is probably significant that the porcupines are hurt by the quills only of those porcupines that are closest to them. The porcupine that's far away doesn't cause pain, nor does it provide any warmth. It is good to remember that in life, the little heartaches and the odd discomfort and pain may be caused by the ones closest to us—but they are the ones who give us warmth when we need it most.

So while porcupines naturally like to keep their distance and avoid getting hurt by each other's quills, it takes a severe winter to bring them all together. Good leaders ensure there is a winter on the horizon—it binds the team together. Without this, minor differences and sharp edges are magnified and threaten to pull the team apart. But faced with the prospect of a winter, the team rallies together, recognizing it as the only way to overcome the external threat.

At the peak of the cola wars in India, Pepsi and Coke both discovered that passions were running high in their organizations. It was a war out there, and the teams found themselves bonding over stories of failure and triumph. There was a common enemy out there—and that seemed to give a purpose to their existence. In fact it was rumoured that a senior planner in Coke once remarked—only half in jest—'If there were no Pepsi, we would have had to invent it!' An in-your-face enemy may keep you up all night, but he also provides a rallying point that binds the team together.

It is also wrong to believe that great teams are always made up of perfectly compatible folks and that all the teammates gel well. That is seldom the case. The key is to learn to live with the other person's imperfections—quills and all—and look at the good they can do, and value the warmth they can provide. That's what great teams are all about.

The next time you get irritated by the minor imperfections of a colleague or friend think of those as the quills of a porcupine that's close to you—and remind yourself of the winter that may lie ahead.

Getting away from people is easy. Surviving alone is tough.

It is good to remember that in life, the little heartaches and the odd discomfort and pain may be caused by the ones closest to us—but they are the ones who give us warmth when we need it most.

The Elephant's Trunk and the Mahout's Stick

Have you heard the story of the mahout and the temple elephant? In a small town in Kerala, there was a temple elephant who was very much the local hero, often revered and always loved.

Every day, the elephant would be taken out for a stroll through the lanes of the busy bazaar. As it walked along, the elephant would do as it pleased. It would reach out with its trunk for a bunch of bananas hanging in front of a store, and before the hapless shopkeeper could react, the bananas would be inside the elephant's mouth. It would sway its trunk into another store, and bring down bunches of carefully arranged flowers. Or it would grab a coconut from the woman selling coconuts on the road and crunch it in its mouth like a walnut. The mahout would try and stop the elephant from doing all this, but to no avail. The mahout even tried beating the elephant with his stick, but it wouldn't listen. The bananas and the coconuts were just too tempting to resist.

And then one day, the clever mahout had an idea. As the elephant was leaving the temple gates for its evening walk, the mahout held his stick out for the elephant to hold with its trunk. The elephant obediently took the mahout's stick and curled its trunk around it.

Now, as it walked through the busy bazaar street, the elephant longingly eyed the bananas but since it held the stick with its trunk, it left the fruits alone. To grab the bananas, it would have to drop the stick—and that would mean offending the mahout. So the elephant held on to the stick that the mahout had given it and walked through the street without disturbing the merchandise in the shops. The shopkeepers were delighted, their admiration for the temple elephant grew, and they often handed over gifts for the elephant to the mahout.

If you think about it, we are all a bit like the elephant. As we go through our lives, we get distracted by the temptations around us. And even though our mahouts—our parents, our teachers and our bosses—tell us to stay focused and not get distracted, we continue to do so. We spend time watching television shows, surfing the Net aimlessly, sleeping the extra hour and chatting non-stop. What we really need is that stick to hold. And that stick is usually a goal—a purpose—that excites us and keeps us on track. Once you have identified a goal in life, you suddenly find yourself focused on doing everything it takes to achieve it. Like an elephant's trunk, our minds too wander. We need that stick to keep it focused.

Have you ever been told, 'Don't do that' when you were doing something you shouldn't be doing? Remember how you still went ahead and did it? So the best way to stop a person from doing something she shouldn't be doing is to give her something else to do. Don't want to watch too much TV? Get yourself a good book to read. Don't want to eat another pack of those chips? Eat a fruit.

A problem confronting many organizations today is the increasing amount of time employees seem to be spending at work surfing social networking sites. Some leaders have responded by restricting access to sites such as Facebook, Gmail and so on with a view to stopping employees from wasting work hours. Does it help? You know it doesn't. For a start, employees feel bitter about what they perceive to be a harsh, unfriendly company policy. And then, they soon figure out circuitous ways to work around the embargo to access the 'banned' websites. Clearly, beating employees with a stick does not work.

Good leaders recognize that the solution lies in ensuring that employees have real work to do. Goals to achieve, timelines to meet and a purpose at work that keeps them focused on the task at hand. And when that happens—when they have a stick to hold in their trunks—they find they have no time to waste chatting and surfing those social networking sites!

Most of our problems in life start when we don't have anything meaningful to do. Having no goals means not having to work towards achieving them. You need the stick—in all areas of your life, not just at work. Not having a hobby or a passion means spending long hours doing nothing. That old adage still rings true—an idle mind is indeed a devil's workshop.

So starting today, get yourself a goal, a purpose that drives you to action. That's not all. Play a sport, indulge a passion, spend time on a hobby—don't just sit there doing nothing. Unlike the temple elephant, not all of us are lucky enough to find a mahout—a caring leader—who gives us that stick to hold. But we all need that goal!

You'll find a stick for yourself today, won't you? And as a leader, make sure your teammates too have a stick to hold.

As we go through our lives, we get distracted by the temptations around us. To stay focused and not get distracted, what we need is a goal—a purpose—that excites us and keeps us on track. Once you have identified a goal in life, you suddenly find yourself focused on doing everything it takes to achieve it.

Having no goals means not having to work towards achieving them.

The Disaster at Angers Bridge!

The army has always been a terrific metaphor for teams in the corporate world. Military life is full of fascinating stories of leadership and teamwork. And discipline is often the hallmark of all those great endeavours. We've all heard stories of how the leader's wish was the team's command—'Theirs not to reason why, theirs but to do and die'.

Leaders love the stuff about discipline and obedience. If you eavesdrop on a boardroom discussion, you will almost always find a leader feeling great when his team echoes his strategies and ideas. There's a word for it—often misused—'alignment'. That's the feeling of having everyone agree with the team leader's ideas. A leader recognizes that unless his team is in sync—in alignment—execution of the strategy will suffer. So alignment is critical once an action plan has been agreed upon. But seeking it too soon can often mean that a team is headed down the wrong path—albeit in complete alignment!

How a leader responds to the dissenting voice can often be the true mark of leadership greatness. Does he snub the dissenting voice? Is the rebel made to feel like the non-aligned guy, the perennial doubter? Or does the leader embrace the dissenter and strive to understand his point of view? Do leaders recognize the power of the dissenting voice?

While all leaders realize the need to allow opposing viewpoints to be debated and discussed, they often subconsciously create an environment where falling in line is seen by the team as the convenient, preferred option. As a subordinate speaks up to express his opinion, the leader begins to squirm uncomfortably and tends to present the examples of the other folks in the room—who are 'aligned' to his viewpoint. It immediately creates an atmosphere of 'who's right' versus 'what's right'. And that snuffs out the debate. Mind you, this is not always intended, but over time this becomes the behaviour into which the team lapses. The advantage of having a team of leaders lies in their collective wisdom, and often colossal mistakes and errors of strategy can be avoided by engaging the whole group and leveraging its pool of intelligence and experience. By suppressing that, leaders weaken themselves. It's one thing to seek alignment after a decision is taken. It's quite another to seek alignment without healthy debate. Simply put, there are times when you need alignment. And times when you don't.

There's a little known story involving an army of soldiers that may hold an important leadership lesson for us. It's the story of what happened one stormy night way back in 1850 on Angers Bridge over the River Maine in France.

Angers Bridge is still remembered for that tragic night of 15 April 1850, when it collapsed under the weight of 478 French soldiers who were marching across it. There was a thunderstorm that night, and the strong gusts of wind made the suspension bridge sway from side to side. As the soldiers marched together in complete harmony, matching step for step, they caused the bridge to vibrate and oscillate even more. And, as a result of the resonance, the anchoring cable got dislodged from the concrete mooring. The bridge came crashing down. As many as 226 soldiers died in what came to be known as the Angers Bridge tragedy. Though the collapse occurred during a thunderstorm, engineering experts were convinced that it was the cadence—the synchronized steps—of the marching soldiers and not the storm that had caused it. And since that day, it's become a practice for armies to break step when they are crossing a bridge. They are encouraged, nay, mandated, not to march in lockstep whilst crossing a bridge.

Leaders around the world would do well to take a leaf out of the Angers Bridge tragedy. Even in a discipline-driven organization like the army, there are times when it must break step. Dissonance is vital, as the soldiers must not all fall in line. An army marching in unison is a great spectacle and represents the power of disciplined teamwork. But equally, there are times when marching in that manner can prove deadly. The soldiers need to break step. Failure to do that can often spell doom.

As a leader, it seems natural to assume that the team must be disciplined in its execution of tasks. But leaders must also remember that there will be times when we need to cross our own Angers Bridge. Allow dissent and make room for dissonance.

Your team will only emerge stronger. And guess what, so will you.

A leader recognizes that unless his team is in alignment, execution of the strategy will suffer. But seeking alignment too soon can often mean that a team is headed down the wrong path—albeit in complete alignment!

It's one thing to seek alignment after a decision is taken. It's quite another to seek alignment without healthy debate. How a leader responds to the dissenting voice can often be the true mark of leadership greatness.

'Upar se Sirf Gap hi Gap Nazar Aata Hai!'

Viren Rasquinha is a man of many parts. A former captain of the Indian hockey team, he's also an Olympian, an alumnus of the prestigious Indian School of Business, and now the CEO of Olympic Gold Quest. It is an organization that's helping to make champion sportspeople in India. At a Coaching Conclave organized by the Coaching Foundation of India, I had the privilege of being on a panel with Viren, trying to pick his brains on what executive coaches could learn from sports coaches. Viren was humility personified, and couldn't resist a chuckle as he recalled two turning points in his life.

The first was when he was passing out of school. He was a good student, and when he scored high marks and topped his school, everyone expected him to get into an engineering college. After all, his mother was a doctor and both his brothers were engineers. But by then the hockey bug had bitten young Viren, and he was tempted to chase his dream and give the sport a shot. When he chose hockey over studies, everyone was surprised.

And then, at age twenty-eight, came the next turning point. At the peak of his playing career, he decided to give it all up to pursue an MBA at the Indian School of Business in Hyderabad. When he chose studies over hockey, again, needless to say, everyone was surprised!

As someone who has played sport at the highest level—he led the India team—and then moved into a CEO role, Viren knows a thing or two about leadership and coaching people. He loves to narrate a tale from his playing days that holds a valuable lesson for leaders and coaches in every field of life.

It was a day of practice for the India team before an important game against the Aussies. Coach Cedric D'Souza was in charge and he was going through recorded footage of an earlier game, sharing expert advice. He was a good coach, much respected, and one of the first to use video analysis in training. As they watched the game on the big screen, the team saw Mukesh Kumar—India's star forward—dribbling his way towards the Aussie goal—but instead of hitting it into a gap, he hit it straight to an Australian defender. The coach hit the pause button at just that instant and said to Mukesh: '*Dekho*! *Itne saare gap thhe—aur tumne seedha unke player ko pass kiya*! (Look! There were so many gaps—and yet you passed the ball straight to an opponent!)'

Mukesh turned to his coach and asked him to rewind the tape. And as the sequence played out, Mukesh said to his coach: '*Sir, upar se sirf gap hi gap nazar aata hai. Neeche aake dekho to kuch aur hi nazar aayega*! (From up above, all you see are gaps everywhere. On the actual field of play the reality is very different!)'

What is true of the game of hockey is true across businesses too. Leaders and coaches would do well to remember that they need to relate to other people—at their level. The distance between a leader and a subordinate may not be too great on an organization chart but the perspectives can be very, very different. Good leaders learn to put themselves in their teammates' shoes. The view from the top is often distorted. Good leaders never forget that '*Upar se sirf gap hi gap nazar aata hai*!'

As I heard Viren recount the story, I was reminded of my days at Pepsi. My mind went back to those innumerable market visits. We'd be out meeting dealers and visiting stores, and the script would be the same for most visits. Typically, the sales guys would have slogged to ensure that our products were available in as many stores as possible. They'd also make sure every store had at least a few bottles of even the less popular, slower moving brands. The salesman would be doing his bit to help his company win the war. But as leaders, what would we notice? We'd see a small shop somewhere selling soft drinks—but no Pepsi. And we'd point out the huge opportunity we were missing! We'd spot some shop that would have Pepsi but no Mirinda. And we'd talk about the missed sales opportunity. It now strikes me that we could see only the missing pieces—the gaps! And there was little or no appreciation for the effort put in to ensure that Pepsi was everywhere. Well, almost everywhere. And as all those images from the past raced through my mind, I wished I had heard Viren's story earlier!

When the hockey coach pointed out the gaps to Mukesh Kumar that day, he was falling into two common leadership traps. One, failing to appreciate the good work done—after all, Mukesh had dribbled the ball past several opponents to get close to the Australian goal. And two, failing to realize that in that moment, all that Mukesh could probably see were the Aussie giants in yellow and green!

As leaders, we often fall into the trap of wanting to dish out advice and point out the flaws. We should take some time out to understand the real picture before coming up with our master solutions to the problem.

The next time you think you've spotted an obvious flaw in a colleague's work—or the missing piece in a team member's output—take a deep breath before you take off. Don't rush to tell him what's wrong. First, try and appreciate the work done. Put yourself in his shoes. And try and look at the problem from that perspective.

And remember, *upar se sirf gap hi gap nazar aata hai*!

The distance between a leader and a subordinate may not be too great on an organization chart but the perspectives can be very, very different. Good leaders learn to put themselves in their teammates' shoes. The view from the top is often distorted. Good leaders never forget that '*Upar se sirf gap hi gap nazar aata hai*!'

Of Tappers and Listeners

In 1990, a psychology student at Stanford University conducted an interesting experiment. It was referred to as the 'Tappers and Listeners' experiment. The rest of the world first heard of it when the authors Chip and Dan Heath started talking about it in public.

For her PhD dissertation, Elizabeth Newton invited her peers in college to participate in the study. Each student was assigned one of two roles: 'tapper' or 'listener'. The tappers were given a list of twenty-five popular tunes, such as *Happy birthday to you* and *Jingle bells*. They had to tap out the tune with their fingers on a table, and the listeners had to guess the song. As you might have guessed, this was not an easy task at all. Of the hundred-and-twenty times that a tune was tapped, the listener could guess the tune correctly only thrice. That's a success rate of about 2.5 per cent.

But here's the interesting bit. Before the tappers began to tap the tune, Elizabeth asked them to predict the probability of the listeners being able to guess the song correctly. The tappers predicted a 50 per cent chance that they would be able to get the listeners to guess the tune correctly.

So while they thought that they would be able to get the listeners to guess correctly one out of two times, the reality was that listeners could guess the tune only once in forty attempts. How come?

Well, here's what was happening. As the tapper taps the tune, he can hear the song playing in his head. His fingers seem to be tapping the tune in perfect sync with what's playing in his head. And he just can't understand why the listener is not able to pick up such a simple tune!

And what about the listener? Well, she doesn't have the tune playing in her head, without which, she has no idea what's happening. She tries as hard as she can to make sense of the bizarre Morse-code like tapping that she hears. Alas, to no avail. This results in utter frustration.

As leaders, we often fall into the tappers' trap! We give instructions which seem very clear in our heads but our colleagues may have no idea what we want them to do. Has it happened to you that you called in a young trainee to do some work, and when she got back the next day—having slogged all night to finish the task—you were disappointed? She hadn't quite done what you were looking for. You probably felt a bit frustrated too, that she 'didn't quite get it'.

The next time that happens, do remember that the problem is with the tapper—not the listener. Because you knew what you wanted to get done, you assumed it was clear to the young trainee too. That is seldom the case.

The tappers and listeners story plays out with several senior leaders too when they issue statements that sound cryptic to employees. The CEO says, 'Our vision is to build shareholder value'. And to the engineer in the factory or the sales guy out in the frontline, that vision means nothing. Zilch! 'Shareholder value? What's that got to do with what I am doing?' he wonders.

The next time you are communicating with a colleague, think about the 'Tappers and Listeners' experiment. And remember, what's obvious to you may not be so to the other person. When the listener says he doesn't get it, that's not a signal to get irritated. It's probably telling you to put yourself in the other person's shoes, and try and be more explicit. Don't assume that knowledge levels are the same.

One more thing. Tapping harder or tapping repeatedly won't make it any easier for the listener!

The next time you are communicating with a colleague, remember, what's obvious to you may not be so to the other person. When the listener says he doesn't get it, that's not a signal to get irritated. It's probably telling you to put yourself in the other person's shoes, and try and be more explicit.

A Very, Very Special Lesson from Laxman

In the pantheon of Indian cricket stars, there will always be a special place for V.V.S. Laxman. Who can forget the Kolkata Test against the marauding Australians! His 281 in the second innings—with India following on—is widely regarded as the finest Test innings by an Indian cricketer. More importantly, it helped India craft an unlikely win. Laxman may never have captained the India team, but there is a terrific leadership lesson that one can take away from the batting heroics of the great Hyderabadi—his ability to bat with tail-enders, people far less capable of scoring runs than he was.

As leaders, we often complain about having to deliver results with weak teams, with subordinates who are not as good as ourselves. And if you've ever felt that way, you should hear about the Laxman–Ishant Sharma partnership in Mohali.

The year was 2010. It was another one of those epic India versus Australia encounters. Riding on a hundred from Shane Watson, Australia scored 428 in their first innings. India replied with 405 runs, Tendulkar top-scored with 98. And then Ishant Sharma and Zaheer Khan got into the act claiming six wickets between them to have Australia all out for 192. That left India with an eminently gettable target of 216 to win the Test.

Gettable did I say? Well it didn't seem that way soon after, when Gautam Gambhir was out without scoring, and India were zero for one after the first over. Wickets fell at regular intervals, and since he was nursing a bad back, Laxman only came in to bat at the fall of the fifth wicket. It was 76 for 5 when Laxman walked in with a runner. After a brief partnership with Tendulkar, who soon departed, wickets fell in a heap again and India was staring at defeat with the scoreboard reading 124 for 8. Ishant Sharma walked out to join V.V.S. Laxman. They had 92 runs to get, 2 wickets in hand. And as commentators would have loved to say, it was all over bar the shouting.

To cut a long story short, V.V.S. made an unbeaten 73, Ishant a valiant 31 and India won the Test match with a wicket to spare. Against all odds, Laxman had shepherded India to a famous victory. What marked Laxman's knock as special was not the fact that he braved back pain and a hostile attack to take India to victory with just batsmen Nos. 10 and 11 for company. It was the way he batted with the tail-enders.

Most batsmen in such situations keep as much of the strike as possible, fearing that their partners won't be good enough to last more than a ball or two. It is quite normal to see batsmen refuse a single in the early part of the over so as to retain strike. And then they try very hard to get a single in the latter part of the over to retain strike in the next over.

But what does Laxman do? Just the opposite. He bats with complete disregard for the fact that he has tail-enders for company. He entrusts them with batting responsibly to the best of their abilities.

In each of the first six overs in their partnership, Laxman faced the first ball taking a single each time—potentially exposing Ishant to facing five deliveries. And Ishant responded in style, confidently playing the bowling! This attitude continued for the duration of the partnership that lasted 22 overs; Laxman faced the first ball of an over nineteen times. And in fifteen of those, he took a run off the first ball, trusting his less gifted partner to rise to the occasion.

Laxman seemed to be telling Ishant he could do it. Every tail-ender cherishes his batting abilities and dreams of winning a game with the bat!

As leaders we often find ourselves saddled with teams that are 'not quite as good'. We complain about their inadequacies, almost seeking martyrdom for our efforts in the face of our team's limitations. In such situations, it is not uncommon to find the leader striving to do other people's work, or in some cases, all the work. Simply because we believe our team is not good enough. We complain by offering our team's limitations as the reason for our inability to deliver results. Sounds familiar? Working with a team that may not be seen as capable is perhaps akin to a frontline batsman having to bat with tail-enders. As leaders we need to take a leaf out of Laxman's textbook, and learn to trust our teammates.

When you trust your team and back them to succeed, there is an all-round rise in confidence levels. The team's desire to live up to that faith only strengthens. And with a point to prove, they deliver results that are spectacular—and surprising.

So the next time you feel you have a team that's not as strong as you'd like, don't complain. Don't try and be a hero and do it all yourself. Don't take actions that only serve to remind the teammates of their incapability. Instead, wave the Laxman wand. Challenge them, inspire them, guide them, push them—but trust them. Let them know you are backing them to do a great job. Lead the way, but allow them to be a part of the challenge.

In an illustrious career spanning over sixteen years, Laxman wore the India colours with great distinction. And while we celebrate his craftsmanship and his valiant efforts, we tend to forget that many of his match-winning innings came batting at No. 6, often with only tail-enders for company. Trusting your seemingly less capable teammates, willing them on, and backing them to succeed can pay rich dividends. For them. For you. And for your team.

The next time you feel you have a team that's not as strong as you'd like, don't complain. Don't try and be a hero and do it all yourself. Don't take actions that only serve to remind the teammates of their incapability. Instead, challenge them, inspire them, guide them, push them—but trust them. Let them know you are backing them to do a great job. The team's desire to live up to that faith only strengthens. And with a point to prove, they deliver results that are spectacular—and surprising.

The Truck with No Tail Lights

Have you been on the Mumbai–Pune Expressway? It's a beautiful stretch of road, about 100 kilometres long, with the Western Ghats providing a scenic backdrop. It's one of the nicest stretches to drive on in India. And, as I learned while on the road one night, it can also teach you a lesson or two about leadership and human behaviour.

While the drive during the day allows you to savour the many shades of green as you cruise along, the drive at night can become a little more mysterious as you try and make sense of the silhouettes. And the drive at night can be much slower too—punctuated by the many trucks that seem to be crawling ahead of you, struggling to pull their weight over the hills of Lonavala.

On a night-time drive sometime ago, there was something dangerously amiss about the trucks that caught my attention. Many of those heavy vehicles had virtually no functioning tail lamps. So it often happened that from behind, you could not tell there was a vehicle in front of you—until you got perilously close! Interestingly enough, all the trucks had functioning headlights, so the truck driver could clearly see what was ahead of him. But having no rear lights meant that the folks driving behind him had a problem. The truck driver or the owner, in his wisdom and cost-cutting prudence, had focused on the light ahead because *he* needed it. And ignored the tail lamps possibly rationalizing that it was *someone else's* problem! The headlights were something he could see. The tail lamps were out of sight, and out of mind.

And that set me thinking. In our lives, do we all behave like those truck drivers? Do we do all the stuff that's good for us—fix our headlights—and ignore what might impact others and be of help to them? Do we forget to check if our tail lamps are functioning? Do we get caught up in achieving our goals and not bother about helping other people achieve theirs?

Good leaders make sure they have great headlights—and excellent tail lamps too. They recognize that there are folks behind them who need to see those tail lamps as they drive forth on their journey. It's a poor leader who is solely focused on his own bosses, constantly looking up, and forgetting about the people he leads, the people who are counting on the tail lamps.

Not having tail lamps can cause an accident and interrupt the journey. And when that happens, it doesn't really matter whether you get hit from the front or from the back. Not having functioning tail lamps is as bad for the truck as it is for the vehicles behind it.

Think of the tail lamps in your life as those acts and little things that help other people more than they help you. Make sure you have an attitude that recognizes the utility of those tail lights. And think of the tail lamps as the things that you know exist but don't always see. Just because you can't see them—or won't be around to see them—does not make them any less important.

Several sales managers are guilty of bending, nay breaking, the system to achieve their targets. They are bright, ambitious folks, target-driven to a fault, and unfortunately, find themselves too caught up in achieving their own short-term goals. So to ensure that their stint is marked by record-breaking numbers, they beat the system, damage distributor and trade relationships, overshoot their budgets, put undue pressure on their sales teams and destroy morale—but they sure get their targets for the quarter, or even the year. They get promoted and move on to a better role or a new job. Their focus is solely on the headlights and not on the tail lamps.

And then someone else comes in to take their place, saddled with the task of repairing the damage. The sales manager who caused it all thought he wouldn't be around to see it, so why bother! Truth is, word soon spreads that he is a truck without tail lamps!

When you are not achieving your goals, the feedback is instantaneous. You can see yourself falling behind. It's like that with your headlights—when one of them malfunctions—you know it as soon as you drive in the dark.

But that's not the case with your tail lights. If you don't check regularly, it could be a long time before you figure out they have stopped working. And chances are, none of the drivers behind you will overtake you to let you know that your tail lights aren't working.

While on the subject of overtaking, here's another thought. You have the bullies and the blockers on the road—you know, the ones who don't allow folks behind them to overtake them. And then you have the other drivers who recognize that someone behind them is clearly driving at a pace that's faster, and make way for him. As a leader, be like that! Recognize when a follower is making rapid progress and is ready to get ahead. Don't be a blocker. Use your tail lights to indicate that it is okay for him to overtake and get ahead! Chances are, the follower will be grateful to you forever!

So as a good leader, make it a habit to check your tail lights! Does the team see you as caring for them? Can they see the path you are leading them on? Do they see the light ahead? That's what good leaders are all about.

You have a choice. You could either be the 'headlights only' leader, focusing solely on who's ahead of him, or you could be the guy with the headlights and the tail lamps, who knows where he is going and cares for those following him. Which would you rather be?

As you drive along on the leadership journey, do occasionally pause to check and make sure your vehicle is in good shape. And when you do that, make sure that both the headlights and the tail lamps are in working condition.

Good leaders make sure they have great headlights—and excellent tail lamps too. They recognize that there are folks behind them who need to see those tail lamps as they drive forth on their journey. It's a poor leader who is solely focused on his own bosses, constantly looking up, and forgetting about the people he leads, the people who are counting on the tail lamps. Think of the tail lamps in your life as those acts and little things that help other people more than they help you.

Going for the Jugular!

It's a phrase with an almost magical ring to it. Not surprisingly, we hear it often in boardrooms and on corporate battlefields. I am guessing it wasn't too long ago that you heard a leader say, 'Let's go for the jugular!' Sales armies and marketing generals are all regularly exhorted to go for the kill.

The phrase immediately brings to life the image of a cheetah going for the kill. Juxtaposed with an image of the poor deer having run as fast as it possibly could, finally seeing its end draw near, struggling for life as the cheetah's jaws snap at its neck, spelling instant death. The phrase owes its origin to the belief that an animal often kills another by biting into the jugular vein—the vein in the neck that carries blood to the heart—causing the poor prey to bleed to death.

But here's the interesting bit. As the cheetah sets out on the breathless chase to catch its prey, guess which part of the deer the cheetah actually targets? No, it's not the jugular. The cheetah does not even think of it. It sets its eyes instead on the deer's legs. More specifically, the hind legs! The cheetah knows that the deer is a quick runner, and catching up and 'going for the jugular' will never be easy. So the clever cheetah aims for the hind legs of the deer. That's the closest. And it knows that once it sinks its teeth into the deer's leg, the deer will not be able to run as quickly. A bite on the leg—and the deer instantly loses its ability to speed. Getting 'the jugular' then becomes a much simpler task.

As leaders set goals for themselves and for their teams, they should remember the cheetah's strategy. Don't go for the jugular. Aim instead for the hind legs! Aiming for the ultimate prize—the jugular—might make the task seem more difficult and harder to achieve. Set an intermediate goal, and attaining that might actually help accelerate the achievement of the long-term goal.

Imagine you are a No. 2 player in the soft drinks business in a territory. You are available in 70 per cent of all soft drink selling outlets and have a 35 per cent share of the market (vis-à-vis the market leader, which has a 60 per cent share and is present in 95 per cent of the universe of outlets). As a fresh young leader you might want to set your team the audacious target of overtaking the market leader and becoming No. 1. It would excite the team for sure, because they see in it the aggression of a leader 'going for the jugular'. But in reality, the road is likely to be long and hard, and there is a real danger that the team might feel frustrated and give up long before the target is near.

Aim for the hind leg: in this case, aim to increase the width of distribution and match the leader. Now that's an easier fix. And once you go from 75 per cent distribution width to 95 per cent, market leadership seems so much more doable!

It's the same with your personal goals. Instead of focusing on the large jugular varieties (I want to be a millionaire, or I want to be CEO, or . . . take your pick!), aim for an intermediate goal, a closer, more achievable target. And you will find that once you achieve that, success seems within reach. You will find yourself accelerating towards the achievement of your ultimate goals.

It's a strategy that works in sports too. Remember Nasser Hussain, the England captain, getting his spinner to bowl outside leg stump to Sachin Tendulkar? The jugular—the ultimate goal—was of course to get Sachin out. Never an easy task! But the hind leg strategy was to get the England spinners to bowl outside leg stump, dry up the runs, frustrate Tendulkar, and force him to manufacture shots and attempt something silly. Leading naturally to the ultimate goal!

If you are unhappy with that bulge at your waist, and how every time you step on the scales it shows you weigh ten kilos more than you should, what do you do? Many of us go for the jugular—and declare our intent to lose ten kilos! And if you've tried that—like I have—

you'll know it seldom works. A more effective approach would be to aim for diet control and say no to carbs after 7 p.m. Or to get into a physical exercise regimen and target to spend thirty minutes on the treadmill at least five times a week. Do either of the two and you will be well on your way to knocking off those ten kilos!

The next time you are setting a goal for yourself or your team, think of the cheetah. And remember, going for the jugular surely sounds sexier. But it's aiming for the hind leg which is usually the more effective strategy.

Aiming for the ultimate prize—going for the jugular—might make the task seem more difficult and harder to achieve. Set an intermediate goal, and attaining that might actually help accelerate the achievement of the long-term goal. Remember the cheetah's strategy. Don't go for the jugular. Aim instead for the hind legs!

The Pencil and the Eraser

There's an interesting story of an imaginary conversation between a pencil and an eraser.

'I am sorry,' said the pencil to the eraser.

'Whatever for?' asked the eraser.

'I am sorry as you get hurt because of me,' continued the pencil. 'Every time I make a mistake, you are there to erase it. And every time you erase one of my mistakes, you lose a bit of yourself. You become smaller and smaller. And just a bit dirty too.'

'You shouldn't really worry,' responded the eraser. 'I was meant to help you whenever you made a mistake, and I am happy doing my job. And I know one day I'll be gone and you will find someone else to do my job, but while I am around, I take pride in knowing I did my bit to help erase your mistakes. Keep writing. Remember, never be scared to make a mistake. There will always be an eraser around to set it right!'

Give it a thought: you'll probably recognize that our teachers were the erasers early on in our lives. We were the pencils—sharp, pointed and colourful. Every time we made a mistake, our teachers were there to correct us. They gave a bit of themselves—so that we could emerge looking just a bit better. And as we moved from school to college and then to work, we found new teachers. But there is no overlooking the fact that we are what we are today, because of those teachers, those wonderful, magical erasers.

That conversation between the pencil and the eraser could well be a conversation between a corporate leader and a protégé, a mentor and a mentee. Good leaders never forget that one of the key roles they play is that of a teacher. Folks who help young managers become great pencils, who erase mistakes and help the pencil's work look good. Most importantly, good leaders are the ones who give their subordinates the freedom and the confidence to make mistakes—secure in the knowledge that they are around to correct them and help them up if they stumble.

There's another thing about teachers that makes them truly special. Their ability to look at every student, every child, and see the genius inside. They know that each child is different and that there is a unique skill or strength inside each and every one of them. I recall a friend telling me about an interaction she had with her children's schoolteacher several years ago. The teacher's words remain etched in her mind to this day.

My friend was worried about her second son, who

wasn't getting the kind of grades that his elder brother was. He didn't seem to be studying enough, his grades were poor, his math skills were weak and, like any parent, she was worried about her son's future. When she raised the issue of her son's performance, here's what the teacher told her: 'Don't worry about his grades. He's an extremely popular, well-adjusted kid. You can't expect mangoes to grow on a guava tree. Different trees bear different fruits. Enjoy each fruit. Parents and teachers—we are just the gardeners. Our job is to water the plant, give it nourishment and allow it to grow into a healthy tree.' And guess what? Both those boys have grown up to be fine young men who are successful in their own right in different fields.

Good leaders don't see themselves as people who manufacture a certain type of leader. They don't try and make their team look 'just like themselves'. They don't force their own style on their teammates. Instead, what they do is allow the genius inside every individual to flower and find expression. They help other people become the best they can be. They recognize that mangoes don't grow on guava trees.

And so every September when the world celebrates Teachers' Day, maybe we should spare a thought for all leaders too—those fabulous, selfless human beings who make a difference to our lives. Let's thank those men and women—all those teachers—who happily got a little dirtier to keep us clean, who didn't mind losing a bit of themselves to make our work error-free. And who were happy to fade away and watch our work with pride as we moved on to newer worlds, and newer teachers. The pencils might get all the glory and acclaim, but it's good to remember that it's the erasers who made it all possible.

As a Teachers' Day special, do yourself a favour. Pick up a pencil. And send a message to an old teacher or leader to thank him or her for being that wonderful eraser in your life.

After all, every eraser was once a pencil!

'You shouldn't really worry,' said the eraser to the pencil. 'I was meant to help you whenever you made a mistake, and I am happy doing my job. I know one day I'll be gone, but you should keep writing. Remember, never be scared to make a mistake. There will always be an eraser around to set it right!'

Acknowledgements

A question I often got asked after *The Habit of Winning* was published was how long it took me to write it. And my answer usually was—a lifetime! And now two years later, this second book might have warranted a different response to that question—but if truth be told, the answer remains just the same.

I'd like to thank all those wonderful folks who've touched me in what's been a lifetime full of fun. People I've been privileged to call friend or colleague—and in many cases, friend *and* colleague. I am constantly reminded of the truth in Isaac Newton's words: 'If I have seen further than others, it is because I was standing on the shoulders of giants.' Thanks guys—and girls—for some invaluable lessons, terrific times and wonderful memories.

The vital first break in life is always a big moment—although you don't necessarily see it that way when it happens. For me, it was a small classified ad that did it. It said: 'Copywriter wanted for an ad agency'. I was still in college, not yet old enough to drive—but I gathered my wits (and my collection of letters to the editor of

Sportsweek!) and walked into Gulshen Patel's office in South Mumbai. Not sure what she saw in me, but she hired me as a part-time copywriter for her agency. Knowing that knocking on the door that day opened up an opportunity to spend time doing something I was fond of—and get paid for it—did wonders for my self-belief. Thanks Gulshen, for betting on that unripe fruit, many, many years ago. Since then, I have had the good fortune of working alongside several outstanding leaders who have taught me, moulded me, inspired me and made a difference to my life. To all of them—a big thank you.

Several of the stories and ideas in this book were born in the monthly column I write for *Careers360*. Maheshwer Peri and the team there have given me a platform that allows me to reach out to young people looking for advice and counsel. I must confess that when an email comes in from a reader saying how something I wrote impacted them—it feels good to know that in my own little way, I made a difference. Suddenly, those late nights and tight deadlines and missed dinners with friends seem worthwhile! Thanks Mahesh (Peri and Sarma) and Merril and the readers of *Careers360* for allowing me to be a co-passenger on your journey!

This book gathered momentum when a young man called Anish Chandy came on as my editor at Penguin. His energy, his ideas (and the shared passion for cricket) ensured that the sense of excitement just kept climbing as we worked together on the book. Thanks Anish. And thanks also to my copy editor Arpita Basu who did a fabulous job of ensuring the writing remained conversational yet correct, which also meant allowing several sentences (including this one!) to start with 'And'. Thanks also to Udayan and the entire Penguin team—including Rahul and the Penguin sales army—for making it happen.

Like several people of my generation, I've been a huge fan of Rahul Dravid. An outstanding professional, a thorough gentleman and a complete team-man, Rahul was all that you could ask for in a friend or a colleague. Rahul was always this somewhat unusual cricketer—self-effacing, studious, pushing himself relentlessly to doing the best he possibly could at all times, and forever thinking about the team's interest. For me, Rahul epitomized what true leadership is all about. So when he said he'd enjoyed reading the stories in *The Habit of Winning*—and consented to write the foreword to this book despite a hectic schedule—I was truly delighted. Thanks Rahul. You are an inspiration!

And finally, a big thank you to the three people in my life who make my world go round: my wife and kids. Savvy, Abs and Tuts—thank you for the support, encouragement and feedback (and for putting up with the erratic schedules and the odd tantrum). You know what this book means to me. But you have no idea what the three of you mean to me!

Enjoy the ride. And unleash the leader within!

'The pessimist complains about the wind.
The optimist expects it to change.
The leader adjusts the sails.'

—John Maxwell